Shifting Mindsets: A Practical Guide to Embracing Positivity

CRAIG HOWARTH

Shifting Mindsets

Copyright © 2024

Publisher Name Here

All rights reserved.

Shifting Mindsets

© Copyright 2024 - All rights reserved.

The content contained within this book may not be reproduced, duplicated, or transmitted without direct written permission from the author or publisher.

Under no circumstances will any blame or legal responsibility be held against the publisher or author for any damages, reparations, or monetary losses due to the information contained within this book. Either directly or indirectly.

Legal Notice:

This book is copyright-protected. This book is only for personal use. You cannot amend, distribute, sell, use, quote, or paraphrase any part, or the content within this book, without the consent of the author or publisher.

Disclaimer Notice:

Please note that the information contained within this document is for educational and entertainment purposes only. All efforts have been executed to present accurate, up-to-date, reliable, and complete information. No warranties of any kind are declared or implied. Readers acknowledge that the author is not rendering legal, financial, medical, or professional advice. The content within this book has been derived from various sources; please consult a licensed professional before attempting any techniques outlined in this book.

By reading this document, the reader agrees that under no circumstances is the author responsible for any direct or indirect losses incurred because of the use of the information contained within this document, including, but not limited to, errors, omissions, or inaccuracies.

Shifting Mindsets

Contents

Defining Mindset: Fixed vs. Growth Mindset	17
The Science behind Mindset and Its Influence on Behaviour and Outcomes	18
How Negativity Develops: Social, Environmental, and Psychological Factors	19
The Impact of Negative Thinking on Mental Health, Relationships, and Personal Growth	20
The Mental and Physical Health Benefits of a Positive Mindset	23
How Positivity Impacts Personal Success, Relationships, and Problem-Solving	25
Real-Life Examples of People Who Transformed Their Lives by Changing Their Mindset	27
Evidence-Based Research Supporting the Power of Positivity	28
10 Easy Everyday Tips to Increase Positive Thinking	29
1. How to Identify Your Current Mindset: Recognizing Negative Patterns	35
2. Exercises for Developing Self-Awareness (e.g., Journaling, Mindfulness)	36
3. Understanding the Triggers of Negative Thinking	38
4. How to Accept and Move Past Limiting Beliefs	39
Introduction to Neuroplasticity: How the Brain Can Change	41
Why Neuroplasticity is Important for Positivity	42
How Negative Thought Patterns are Formed	42
Practical Techniques for Rewiring Negative Thought Patterns	42
Daily Habits to Reinforce Positive Thinking	45
Building Mental Resilience to Overcome Setbacks	46
10 Tips for Preparing to Leave a Long-Term Job and Starting Your Own Business	47
Introduction: The Power of Optimism	52
Strategies to Adopt a Positive Outlook in Everyday Situations	52
Learning to Find Opportunity in Challenges	53
The Power of Reframing Negative Thoughts	54

Shifting Mindsets

Techniques to Stop Overthinking and Reduce Anxiety	55
Embracing Optimism as a Way of Life	56
Key Skills of a Long-Serving Police Officer and How They Transition into Business	57
Leveraging Policing Skills for Entrepreneurial Success	61
How to Sell a Service Successfully: A Professional Guide to Success	61
Additional Resources	68
How Your Environment and Social Circle Influence Your Mindset	69
The Power of Environmental Cues	69
Social Influence: The Energy of People around You	70
The Role of Community and Positive Relationships in Sustaining Positivity	71
Building a Supportive Network That Fosters Growth	73
10 Powerful Examples	74
Common Challenges to Shifting to a Positive Mindset	78
How to Tackle Pessimism, Criticism, and Negative Feedback Constructively	80
Dealing with Setbacks and Failures in a Positive Way	81
Strategies to Maintain Positivity during Tough Times	82
The Science of Gratitude and How It Enhances Positivity	84
Practical Exercises for Practicing Gratitude Daily	86
How Mindfulness Helps in Staying Present and Reducing Negative Thinking	87
Building a Gratitude and Mindfulness Routine	88
10 Tips for Financial Freedom: Saving Money, Investing in Yourself, and Building a Future	89
How to Make Positivity a Lifestyle Rather Than a Temporary Phase	95
Creating a Personal Action Plan for Maintaining a Positive Mindset	96
The Role of Continuous Self-Improvement and Reflection	97
Staying Motivated and Consistent in the Journey toward Positivity	99
Creating a Personal Action Plan for Maintaining a Positive Mindset (Continued)	100

Shifting Mindsets

Staying Motivated and Consistent in the Journey toward Positivity (Continued)	102
Aligning Your Mindset with Your Life's Purpose and Values	104
How a Positive Mindset Can Help You Discover and Pursue Your Passion	105
Strategies for Integrating Positivity into All Aspects of Your Life	107
Final Thoughts: Positivity as an Ongoing Journey	108
The Difficulty of Transitioning from Stable Employment	109
The Positive Impact of Being Your Own Boss	110
A Sense of Purpose	112
Bonus Section: Workbook and Exercises	113
Suggested Reading and Resources for Continued Growth	115
Final Words of Encouragement	116

Shifting Mindsets

CHAPTER SUMMARIES

Introduction
- Importance of mindset in shaping our lives
- Overview of the power of positive thinking
- Brief introduction of the author and their personal journey toward a positive mindset
- What readers can expect to gain from the book

Chapter 1: Understanding Mindset
- Defining mindset: Fixed vs. growth mindset
- The science behind mindset and its influence on behaviour and outcomes
- How negativity develops: Social, environmental, and psychological factors
- The impact of negative thinking on mental health, relationships, and personal growth

Chapter 2: The Benefits of Positivity
- The mental and physical health benefits of a positive mindset
- How positivity impacts personal success, relationships, and problem-solving
- Real-life examples of people who transformed their lives by changing their mindset
- Evidence-based research supporting the power of positivity

Chapter 3: Self-Awareness as the First Step
- How to identify your current mindset: Recognizing negative patterns
- Exercises for developing self-awareness (e.g., journaling, mindfulness)
- Understanding the triggers of negative thinking
- How to accept and move past limiting beliefs

Chapter 4: Rewiring the Brain for Positivity
- Introduction to neuroplasticity: How the brain can change
- Practical techniques for rewiring negative thought patterns:
    - Affirmations

- Visualization
- Gratitude journaling
- Positive self-talk
- Daily habits to reinforce positive thinking
- Building mental resilience to overcome setbacks

Chapter 5: Cultivating Optimism in Daily Life
- Strategies to adopt a positive outlook in everyday situations
- Learning to find opportunity in challenges
- The power of reframing negative thoughts
- Techniques to stop overthinking and reduce anxiety

Chapter 6: Surrounding Yourself with Positivity
- How your environment and social circle influence your mindset
- The role of community and positive relationships in sustaining positivity
- How to set boundaries with negativity (people, media, habits)
- Building a supportive network that fosters growth

Chapter 7: Overcoming Obstacles to Positive Thinking
- Common challenges people face when shifting to a positive mindset (e.g., self-doubt, fear, past failures)
- How to tackle pessimism, criticism, and negative feedback constructively
- Dealing with setbacks and failures in a positive way
- Strategies to maintain positivity during tough times

Chapter 8: The Power of Gratitude and Mindfulness
- The science of gratitude and how it enhances positivity
- Practical exercises for practicing gratitude daily
- How mindfulness helps in staying present and reducing negative thinking
- Building a gratitude and mindfulness routine

Chapter 9: Sustaining Long-Term Positivity
- How to make positivity a lifestyle rather than a temporary phase
- Creating a personal action plan for maintaining a positive

mindset
- The role of continuous self-improvement and reflection
- Staying motivated and consistent in the journey toward positivity

Chapter 10: Living a Purpose-Driven Life
- Aligning your mindset with your life's purpose and values
- How a positive mindset can help you discover and pursue your passion
- Strategies for integrating positivity into all aspects of your life (work, relationships, personal goals)
- Final thoughts: Positivity as an ongoing journey

Conclusion
- Recap of key lessons learned
- Encouragement to take small, consistent steps toward a positive mindset
- Final words of motivation: You have the power to change your mindset and, ultimately, your life

Bonus Section: Workbook and Exercises
- Guided journaling prompts
- Daily affirmations
- Gratitude log template
- Mindset tracking sheet
- Suggested reading and resources for continued growth

MY JOURNEY: FROM POLICE OFFICER TO FULL-TIME BUSINESS OWNER

I was a dedicated UK police officer, and embarked on a significant career transformation. After years of serving the public in law enforcement, I transitioned to focus full-time on my passion: running my own company, Evolution K9 Services. My success in making this leap isn't just about skill or timing—it was about my **mindset**.

Leaving behind a stable career in policing for the uncertain world of entrepreneurship is no small feat. For me, the key to success lay in changing my mindset and following fundamental principles similar to those found in the self-help book, "Shifting Mindsets." I realized early on that if I wanted Evolution K9 Services to thrive, I needed to embrace positivity, persistence, and growth-oriented thinking.

Adopting a Growth Mindset
One of the first shifts I made was adopting a **growth mindset**. As a police officer, I was no stranger to problem-solving and facing tough situations, but in business, I had to see every challenge as an opportunity to learn and grow. Instead of fearing the unknowns of entrepreneurship, I viewed them as valuable experiences that would make me better at running my company.

This mindset allowed me to move past self-doubt and embrace the learning curve. I continuously improved my skills, whether through understanding dog behaviour or learning the intricacies of business operations. By believing that my current abilities could develop through hard work and learning, I was able to take calculated risks and push Evolution K9 Services forward.

Positive Thinking in Action
The transition wasn't always easy. There were moments of uncertainty, but my ability to practice **positive thinking** made a crucial difference. Rather than being overwhelmed by setbacks, I focused on solutions and what I could control. This mental shift allowed me to stay motivated and find innovative ways to expand my business.

I applied the principles of positive thinking by surrounding myself with a support network of like-minded individuals who believed in my vision. This positive environment fuelled my confidence and reinforced my decision to leave policing and pursue Evolution K9 Services full-time.

Consistency and Resilience

Another critical factor in this success was his **consistency**. Just as the book emphasizes, making positivity and a growth mindset part of daily routines leads to sustainable change. I incorporated practices like goal-setting, visualization, and reflecting on my progress, helping me stay on track.

Moreover, my resilience—developed through years of policing—enabled me to bounce back from challenges with even more determination. This mindset shift, along with his professional skills, set me on a clear path toward building a successful business.

A Life Transformed

By shifting his mindset and following basic principles of positivity, self-belief, and continuous growth, I not only made a successful transition from law enforcement to entrepreneurship but also turned my passion for working with dogs into a thriving full-time business. My story demonstrates how powerful mindset changes can lead to profound career shifts and personal fulfilment.

Now, with Evolution K9 Services, I am not only pursuing my dream but also helping others through my expertise in dog training. This journey serves as an inspiring example for anyone looking to make a similar transformation in their life or career.

The Power of Mindset: How It Shapes Every Aspect of Our Lives

When you think about success, happiness, and fulfilment, what comes to mind? Most of us consider hard work, talent, or even luck as the driving forces behind achieving our goals. But beneath all of that lies something far more powerful—our **mindset**. It's the lens through which we view the world, the invisible force that directs our actions, decisions, and ultimately, our outcomes.

Mindset isn't just a "feel-good" concept or a motivational buzzword; it's a scientifically backed driver of human behaviour. Whether you're aware of it or not, the way you think about yourself, your potential, and the world around you directly influence the quality of your life. A positive, growth-oriented mindset is the difference between bouncing back from failure or being crushed by it; between seeing opportunity or obstacles; between living with intention or reacting passively to whatever comes your way.

Shifting Mindsets

Mindset: The Foundation of Success

Let's start with one of the most striking findings in psychology: people who believe they can grow and improve are far more likely to succeed than those who think their abilities are set in stone. This is the essence of the *growth mindset*, a term coined by psychologist Carol Dweck. It's not just about being positive; it's about understanding that your talents and intelligence can develop with effort, learning, and persistence.

Think about it—when you believe that you can get better at something, you're more likely to put in the effort required to achieve it. You'll see challenges as opportunities to learn, rather than reasons to give up. On the flip side, a *fixed mindset*, where you believe your abilities are limited or predetermined, can trap you in a cycle of fear and self-doubt, keeping you from even trying.

How Mindset Shapes Your Reality

The power of mindset goes beyond individual success; it determines how you interact with the world. If you approach life with a negative or limiting mindset, you may unconsciously sabotage your own potential. For instance, if you tell yourself, "I'm just not good at public speaking," or "I always fail at relationships," those beliefs become self-fulfilling prophecies. You won't practice your speaking skills or improve your communication, because deep down, you've already accepted defeat.

On the other hand, adopting a positive, growth-cantered mindset rewires your brain to see opportunity where others see limits. Challenges become stepping stones. Failure is not an endpoint, but a valuable lesson on the path to success. Suddenly, what seemed impossible becomes a matter of persistence, strategy, and adaptability. As the saying goes, "Whether you think you can or you think you can't—you're right."

The Ripple Effect on Every Area of Your Life

What makes mindset even more powerful is its ripple effect. It doesn't just impact one area of your life; it touches everything. Your career, relationships, health, and personal happiness are all reflections of your mindset.

Consider your relationships. If you enter relationships believing that conflict equals failure, you might avoid difficult conversations or let resentment build. But with a mindset that views conflict as an opportunity for growth and deeper understanding, you're more likely to engage openly, fostering stronger, more resilient connections.

Shifting Mindsets

In your career, a fixed mindset might make you fear stepping out of your comfort zone or avoid taking risks. Meanwhile, a growth mindset empowers you to take on new challenges, innovate, and continuously evolve. It's the reason why some people thrive in the face of adversity while others falter—they see challenges not as threats but as chances to grow.

The Science Backs It Up
Numerous studies have shown that our mindset directly influences our brain chemistry and physiological responses. People who cultivate a positive mindset experience lower stress levels, better health, and higher overall life satisfaction. Their brains are literally more flexible, open to new ideas, and better equipped to solve problems. In contrast, a negative mindset limits the brain's ability to think creatively or handle stress, leading to a spiral of negativity that reinforces itself.

The good news? Mindset isn't fixed. It's a choice. You have the power to shift your thinking at any moment, and when you do, you begin to unlock doors to opportunities you never thought possible.

Choosing Your Mindset
So, how do you begin the process of reshaping your mindset? It starts with awareness. Pay attention to the stories you tell yourself—the assumptions and beliefs you carry. Are they empowering or limiting? Do they encourage you to grow, or do they keep you stuck?

From there, you can actively cultivate a growth mindset by embracing challenges, learning from criticism, and recognizing that effort is the path to mastery. Surround yourself with people who inspire and uplift you, and make a habit of practicing gratitude, which helps reinforce positivity.

At the end of the day, your mindset is the most powerful tool you have. It's not about being perfect or achieving everything effortlessly; it's about knowing that with the right mindset, anything is possible. And once you make that shift, you'll find that the entire world opens up in ways you never imagined

The Power of Positive Thinking: Unlocking Your Full Potential
Imagine waking up every day feeling energized, confident, and ready to tackle whatever life throws your way. Now, imagine facing challenges with a sense of calm, knowing that, no matter the obstacle, you'll find a way through. This isn't a fantasy or some distant dream reserved for a few lucky people—it's the powerful

result of positive thinking.

The idea that our thoughts can shape our reality might sound simple, but the impact of positive thinking is profound and backed by science. It's not just about putting on a smile or forcing optimism; it's about training your brain to see opportunity where others see obstacles and to approach life with a mindset that fuels success, happiness, and personal growth.

Why Positive Thinking Is So Powerful

At its core, positive thinking is about perspective. It's choosing to see the good in every situation, focusing on solutions rather than problems, and believing that things can, and will, improve. But this isn't just a "feel-good" mantra. Research has shown that how you think has a direct impact on how you experience the world—and the outcomes you achieve.

Here's the kicker: positive thinking doesn't mean ignoring challenges or pretending that life is perfect. It's about developing a mindset that empowers you to respond to life's challenges in a way that keeps you moving forward. When you think positively, your brain literally starts to work differently. It becomes more creative, resilient, and capable of finding solutions that, in a negative state, you might never even notice.

The Science behind Positive Thinking

Studies in psychology and neuroscience have revealed something fascinating—our brains have what's known as a "negativity bias." This means we are naturally wired to focus on threats and dangers. While this helped our ancestors survive, it can cause us to get stuck in cycles of worry, fear, and stress. The good news? We can rewire our brains for positivity.

When you practice positive thinking, it activates the brain's reward centres and increases the release of feel-good chemicals like dopamine and serotonin. These chemicals don't just make you feel happy; they also enhance cognitive function, improving memory, focus, and problem-solving skills. In fact, research shows that positive people are more productive, more resilient, and more likely to achieve their goals.

Turning Setbacks into Stepping Stones

One of the greatest benefits of positive thinking is how it transforms your relationship with failure. In life, setbacks are inevitable. You will face challenges, disappointments, and moments of doubt. But while some people see failure as a dead-end, positive thinkers see it as a

Shifting Mindsets

stepping stone.

With a positive mindset, failure becomes feedback—a valuable lesson that brings you one step closer to success. Instead of getting stuck in frustration or self-blame, you become solution-oriented. You start asking, "What can I learn from this?" and "How can I use this experience to grow?"

This shift in thinking is incredibly powerful. It means that no matter what happens, you have the tools to keep moving forward. Positive thinking becomes a form of mental resilience, helping you bounce back faster and stronger from adversity.

Positive Thinking Is Contagious

Another remarkable aspect of positive thinking is that it's contagious. When you radiate optimism, it affects those around you. Studies show that positivity spreads through social networks like wildfire. It's a phenomenon known as "emotional contagion," where your emotions and attitudes are picked up by those you interact with.

By maintaining a positive outlook, you not only improve your own life but also uplift the people in your personal and professional circles. This ripple effect can lead to stronger relationships, better teamwork, and a more supportive environment wherever you go.

Think about it: Have you ever worked with someone who brought energy and solutions to every challenge? That's the power of positivity in action. When you lead with optimism, you inspire others to do the same, creating a cycle of mutual motivation and success.

How to Cultivate Positive Thinking in Your Life

If positive thinking is so powerful, how do you make it a regular part of your life? It all starts with small, intentional shifts in your mindset and habits. Here are a few practical ways to begin:

1. **Practice Gratitude**: Gratitude is one of the simplest and most effective ways to shift your thinking. By taking time each day to reflect on what's going right, you retrain your brain to focus on the positives, even in tough times. Try keeping a gratitude journal and jot down three things you're thankful for every day.
2. **Reframe Negative Thoughts**: The next time you catch yourself thinking negatively, pause and ask, "Is there another way to look at this?" For example, instead of thinking, "I can't handle this," try reframing it to, "This is tough, but I've faced challenges before and succeeded."

3. **Surround Yourself with Positivity**: The people you spend time with have a huge influence on your mindset. Surround yourself with those who inspire, motivate, and support you. Limit time with people who bring negativity or pessimism into your life.
4. **Focus on Solutions, Not Problems**: When faced with a challenge, train yourself to focus on solutions rather than dwelling on the problem. Ask, "What's one step I can take to improve this situation?" This habit strengthens your problem-solving skills and keeps you moving forward.
5. **Visualize Success**: Spend a few minutes each day visualizing yourself achieving your goals. Picture how it feels, what it looks like, and the steps you took to get there. Visualization primes your brain for success, helping you stay focused and motivated.

The Bottom Line: Positive Thinking Transforms Lives

Positive thinking isn't about ignoring reality or sugar-coating life's difficulties. It's about choosing to focus on what's possible, even when things are hard. It's about believing in your ability to grow, adapt, and overcome. When you commit to thinking positively, you unlock your full potential. You'll find yourself more resilient, more creative, and more confident in your ability to handle whatever life throws your way.

The power of positive thinking lies not in its simplicity, but in its consistency. By making small, daily shifts in your mindset, you can change the trajectory of your life, opening doors to opportunities, success, and happiness that you may never have imagined. So, why not start today? Your best life is waiting—one positive thought at a time.

CHAPTER 1: UNDERSTANDING MINDSET

The concept of mindset, while seemingly straightforward, holds profound implications for personal success, happiness, and growth. At its core, mindset refers to the set of beliefs and attitudes we hold about our abilities, intelligence, and potential. These underlying beliefs shape how we perceive the world, interact with challenges, and respond to failure. Over the past few decades, mindset has become a central focus in both psychology and education, thanks to ground-breaking research by psychologists like Carol Dweck, whose work on *fixed* and *growth* mindsets has revolutionized our understanding of human potential.

Defining Mindset: Fixed vs. Growth Mindset

Mindset can generally be divided into two categories: the **fixed mindset** and the **growth mindset**. These concepts, first introduced by Carol Dweck in her book *Mindset: The New Psychology of Success*, describe how individuals view their intelligence, abilities, and talents.

A **fixed mindset** is the belief that our abilities, intelligence, and talents are static traits—they are something we are born with and cannot change significantly. People with a fixed mindset believe that success is a reflection of inherent talent, and failure is a direct indicator of their limitations. In this mindset, effort is seen as fruitless because success is predetermined by one's natural abilities. As a result, individuals with a fixed mindset tend to shy away from challenges and avoid situations where they might fail, fearing that failure will expose their lack of ability.

In contrast, a **growth mindset** is the belief that our abilities can be developed through dedication, hard work, and learning. People with a growth mindset see challenges as opportunities to improve and view effort as essential for mastery. They understand that failure is not a reflection of their limitations but rather a natural part of the learning process. With a growth mindset, people are more likely to embrace challenges, persist through difficulties, and view feedback and criticism as opportunities for improvement.

Dweck's research revealed that mindset plays a critical role in determining how we approach life's challenges. Individuals with a growth mindset tend to achieve more because they focus on learning and improvement rather than worrying about how they are perceived. In contrast, those with a fixed mindset often limit their potential by avoiding risks and challenges that could lead to growth. This simple shift in belief—from fixed to growth—can have profound effects on one's personal and professional life.

The Science behind Mindset and Its Influence on Behaviour and Outcomes

The power of mindset extends beyond mere philosophy; it has roots in **neuroscience** and psychology. Understanding how mindset affects brain function helps explain why individuals with a growth mindset tend to outperform those with a fixed mindset.

One of the key concepts underlying mindset is **neuroplasticity**, the brain's ability to change and adapt throughout life. For many years, scientists believed that the brain was relatively fixed after early childhood. However, research in recent decades has shown that the brain is highly malleable, capable of forming new neural connections and pathways in response to experiences, learning, and practice. This means that intelligence and abilities are not fixed traits; they can be developed over time with the right approach.

In people with a growth mindset, the brain becomes more responsive to feedback and learning opportunities. Studies using brain imaging have demonstrated that individuals with a growth mindset show greater activation in areas of the brain associated with error correction and learning when faced with a challenge. In contrast, those with a fixed mindset show heightened activity in areas related to emotional responses, such as fear and anxiety, when confronted with the possibility of failure. This difference in brain activity illustrates why growth-minded individuals are more likely to persist in the face of obstacles, while those with a fixed mindset may retreat when faced with difficulty.

A well-known study by Dweck and her colleagues involved giving children puzzles of increasing difficulty. Children with a fixed mindset tended to give up quickly, expressing frustration when they encountered puzzles they couldn't solve easily. However, children with a growth mindset embraced the challenge, showing excitement at the prospect of learning something new—even if it meant initially failing. Their ability to view failure as part of the learning process made them more resilient and persistent.

In the workplace, this mindset can dramatically influence performance and outcomes. Employees with a growth mindset are more likely to take on new challenges, seek out feedback, and adapt to changing circumstances, leading to higher productivity and job satisfaction. Leaders with a growth mindset foster an environment where innovation and creativity thrive, as they encourage their teams to experiment, learn from failure, and continuously improve.

This scientific understanding of how mindset influences behaviour also extends to education. Educators who emphasize effort, improvement, and the learning process can help students adopt a growth mindset, leading to better academic outcomes. In contrast, environments that overly focus on innate talent or grades can reinforce a fixed mindset, limiting students' willingness to take risks or explore new ideas.

How Negativity Develops: Social, Environmental, and Psychological Factors

While mindset is a powerful tool for personal growth, it's important to understand how **negative mindsets** develop. Various social, environmental, and psychological factors can contribute to a fixed or negative mindset, and recognizing these influences is the first step toward breaking free from them.

1. **Social Influences**: From an early age, we are shaped by the messages we receive from those around us—parents, teachers, friends, and society at large. For instance, children who are praised solely for their natural intelligence ("You're so smart!") rather than their effort or process of learning may begin to believe that their abilities are fixed. This can lead to a fear of failure, as they feel the need to protect their "smart" label and avoid challenges that could expose their limitations.

Additionally, societal norms often glorify effortless success. Media frequently highlights prodigies or "overnight" success stories, perpetuating the belief that talent, not effort, is the key to achievement. This creates unrealistic expectations, fostering a fixed mindset in individuals who compare themselves to these narratives.

2. **Environmental Factors**: Our surroundings play a significant role in shaping our mindset. Work environments that punish failure rather than viewing it as a learning opportunity can cultivate a fixed mindset. When employees are constantly evaluated based on results alone, they may avoid taking risks or pursuing innovation out of fear that

failure will harm their career prospects.

In educational settings, a heavy emphasis on grades and standardized testing can lead students to believe that intelligence is fixed and measurable, fostering a fear of failure. These environments often prioritize performance over growth, reinforcing the idea that success is determined by innate talent rather than effort and improvement.

3. **Psychological Factors**: Our psychological makeup and life experiences also contribute to the development of a negative mindset. Traumatic experiences, chronic stress, or a history of repeated failure can reinforce negative beliefs about oneself. Individuals who experience ongoing adversity may develop learned helplessness—a state where they believe their efforts have no impact on their outcomes, leading to a fixed mindset.

Additionally, cognitive biases like **confirmation bias**—the tendency to seek out information that confirms our pre-existing beliefs—can reinforce negative thinking. For example, someone with a fixed mindset may interpret a single failure as proof that they are incapable, ignoring evidence of past successes or areas where they have improved.

By understanding the roots of negativity, we can begin to address these factors and cultivate a more positive, growth-oriented mindset. Awareness of these influences allows us to challenge limiting beliefs and create environments that support growth, learning, and resilience.

The Impact of Negative Thinking on Mental Health, Relationships, and Personal Growth

The effects of negative thinking extend far beyond missed opportunities. Persistent negative thinking can have profound consequences on **mental health, relationships**, and **personal growth**. While it's normal to experience negative thoughts from time to time, allowing these thoughts to dominate your mindset can lead to significant challenges in various areas of life.

1. **Mental Health**: Chronic negative thinking is closely linked to mental health issues such as **anxiety, depression**, and **stress**. When individuals are trapped in a cycle of negative self-talk—such as constantly thinking, "I'm not good enough" or "I'll never succeed"—they can become

overwhelmed by feelings of hopelessness and low self-worth. Over time, these patterns can lead to clinical depression, where individuals feel stuck and unable to make positive changes in their lives.

Furthermore, negative thinking can heighten the body's **stress response**. When we perceive challenges as threats rather than opportunities, our bodies release stress hormones like cortisol, which can negatively impact our physical and mental health. This chronic stress can weaken the immune system, increase the risk of heart disease, and contribute to sleep disturbances, further exacerbating mental health issues.

2. **Relationships**: A negative mindset can also erode personal and professional relationships. Individuals who view themselves or others through a fixed mindset lens may become overly critical, defensive, or resistant to feedback. In relationships, this can manifest as a lack of empathy or an inability to compromise, as those with a fixed mindset may be more focused on proving themselves right than on resolving conflicts constructively.

Moreover, negative thinking can lead to **self-sabotage** in relationships. People who believe they are unworthy of love or success may push others away, engage in toxic behaviours, or avoid vulnerability out of fear of rejection. Over time, this can damage trust, communication, and connection in both personal and professional relationships.

3. **Personal Growth**: Negative thinking is perhaps most destructive when it comes to **personal growth**. Those with a fixed mindset tend to avoid challenges, fearing failure or criticism. This avoidance can prevent individuals from developing new skills, exploring new opportunities, or pursuing meaningful goals. The fear of failure becomes a barrier to growth, locking individuals into a state of stagnation.

By contrast, individuals with a growth mindset view setbacks as temporary and solvable, allowing them to learn from their mistakes and continue moving forward. They embrace challenges, knowing that effort and persistence lead to improvement. This mindset is essential for personal development, as it enables individuals to continually push their boundaries and expand their capabilities.

Shifting Mindsets

Understanding mindset—whether fixed or growth—is critical for unlocking one's potential and achieving success. The science of mindset reveals that our beliefs about ourselves have a powerful influence on our behaviour, outcomes, and overall well-being. By identifying the social, environmental, and psychological factors that contribute to negative thinking, we can begin to break free from limiting beliefs and cultivate a mindset that fosters growth, resilience, and personal development. Whether in the context of mental health, relationships, or personal growth, adopting a growth mindset can transform the way we approach life's challenges, opening the door to new possibilities and greater fulfilment.

CHAPTER 2: THE BENEFITS OF POSITIVITY

Positivity is more than just a pleasant emotional state—it's a powerful force that shapes our reality. A positive mindset not only enhances our personal well-being but also fuels our success, strengthens our relationships, and helps us navigate life's challenges with grace and resilience. In this chapter, we'll explore the profound benefits of positivity, supported by evidence-based research, and dive into real-life examples of individuals who transformed their lives through positive thinking.

The Mental and Physical Health Benefits of a Positive Mindset

A positive mindset has a direct and measurable impact on both mental and physical health. The mind and body are deeply interconnected, and how we think influences how we feel. Numerous studies have demonstrated that individuals who maintain a positive outlook experience better health outcome, live longer, and enjoy greater mental clarity and emotional stability.

1. **Reduced Stress and Anxiety**: One of the most significant mental health benefits of a positive mindset is the reduction of stress and anxiety. When faced with life's challenges, positive thinkers tend to focus on solutions rather than dwelling on the problem. This shift in focus helps them manage stress more effectively. By believing that things will improve and that they have the power to influence outcomes, they experience less anxiety about the future.

    Research conducted by the Mayo Clinic found that individuals with a positive mindset had lower levels of the stress hormone cortisol, which is linked to a variety of health problems, including heart disease, depression, and weakened immune function. By maintaining a positive outlook, people can keep their stress levels in check and enjoy better mental health.

2. **Improved Immune Function**: The benefits of positivity extend to the body's immune system as well. A study published in the journal *Psychosomatic Medicine* found that individuals with a positive mindset had stronger immune responses to infections compared to those with negative

outlooks. This enhanced immune function means that positive people are better equipped to fight off illnesses and recover more quickly from health setbacks.

The mechanism behind this lies in the body's stress response. Chronic negative thinking activates the body's stress response, leading to inflammation and immune suppression. On the other hand, positive emotions like hope, joy, and gratitude promote the release of immune-boosting chemicals and reduce inflammation, improving overall health and vitality.

3. **Longer Life Expectancy**: Positivity has also been linked to longevity. A landmark study conducted by researchers at Yale University found that individuals with a positive outlook on aging lived an average of 7.5 years longer than those with negative attitudes about growing older. This study controlled for factors such as age, gender, socioeconomic status, and physical health, highlighting that mindset plays a crucial role in determining life expectancy.

The reasons for this increased longevity are multifaceted. Positive people tend to engage in healthier behaviours, such as regular exercise, balanced nutrition, and avoiding harmful habits like smoking or excessive alcohol consumption. They are also more likely to seek preventive healthcare and follow medical advice, which contributes to their longer, healthier lives.

4. **Enhanced Emotional Resilience**: Another critical mental health benefit of positivity is increased emotional resilience. Resilience refers to the ability to bounce back from adversity, and individuals with a positive mindset are more likely to recover from setbacks quickly. They are less likely to experience prolonged periods of depression or hopelessness because they focus on the potential for growth and improvement, even in difficult situations.

Positive thinking promotes resilience by fostering a sense of control and optimism. When people believe that they can influence their circumstances, they are more likely to take proactive steps to improve their situation, rather than feeling helpless or defeated. This proactive mindset contributes to better emotional and psychological health, allowing individuals to thrive in the face of challenges.

Shifting Mindsets

How Positivity Impacts Personal Success, Relationships, and Problem-Solving

The benefits of a positive mindset extend beyond health—it also plays a crucial role in personal success, relationships, and our ability to solve problems. Positivity shapes how we approach opportunities, manage conflicts, and handle challenges, leading to more fulfilling and productive lives.

1. Positivity and Personal Success: A positive mindset is one of the most critical factors influencing personal and professional success. Research consistently shows that people who approach life with optimism are more likely to achieve their goals, whether in their careers, education, or personal development.

This success stems from several key attributes associated with positive thinking:

a) **Increased Motivation and Perseverance**: Positive people believe that they can overcome obstacles and succeed, which fuels their motivation to keep pushing forward. When faced with setbacks, they are less likely to give up and more likely to view failure as a learning experience rather than a dead-end. This persistence is a hallmark of successful individuals.

b) **Creative Problem-Solving**: Positivity opens the door to creative problem-solving. When we focus on solutions rather than problems, our brains enter a more expansive, open state. Research from the University of Toronto found that positive emotions broaden our cognitive abilities, allowing us to see new possibilities and think more creatively. This creativity is essential for personal and professional success, as it helps us develop innovative solutions to the challenges we face.

c) **Confidence and Risk-Taking**: Positivity fosters confidence, which is essential for success in any endeavour. When we believe in our abilities, we are more likely to take calculated risks that can lead to growth and achievement. Whether it's starting a new business, pursuing a new career, or embarking on a personal project, confidence derived from positive thinking gives us the courage to step outside our comfort zones and pursue our goals with determination.

1. **Positivity and Relationships**: A positive mindset profoundly influences the quality of our relationships.

Shifting Mindsets

Whether in romantic partnerships, friendships, or professional collaborations, positivity fosters better communication, empathy, and understanding. Here's how:

a) **Improved Communication**: Positive individuals are more likely to engage in open, constructive communication. They focus on finding common ground and resolving conflicts, rather than dwelling on differences or negative aspects of the relationship. This approach leads to healthier, more supportive relationships, as both parties feel heard and understood.

b) **Emotional Contagion**: Positivity is contagious. Research on emotional contagion shows that emotions spread between people in social interactions, influencing the mood and behaviour of others. In relationships, positive emotions like happiness, gratitude, and optimism can lift the mood of others,

c) Creating a cycle of positivity that strengthens bonds. When we radiate positivity, we encourage those around us to adopt a similar mindset, which leads to more harmonious and fulfilling connections.

d) **Resilience in Conflict**: Every relationship experience conflict, but positivity plays a key role in how conflicts are resolved. Positive thinkers approach disagreements with the mindset that problems can be solved through collaboration and understanding. This attitude fosters empathy and patience, allowing both parties to work together to find solutions. In contrast, negative thinking can escalate conflicts, as individuals may become defensive or critical, making resolution more difficult.

2. Positivity and Problem-Solving: One of the most practical benefits of a positive mindset is its impact on problem-solving. Life is full of challenges, but how we approach those challenges determines our success in overcoming them.

a) **Solution-Focused Thinking**: Positive thinkers focus on solutions rather than problems. When faced with a challenge, they ask themselves, "What can I do to improve this situation?" rather than getting stuck in the mindset of "Why is this happening to me?" This solution-focused thinking leads to faster, more effective problem resolution, as it encourages creativity and action.

b) **Reduced Cognitive Biases**: Negativity often leads to cognitive biases, such as **catastrophizing** (expecting the worst possible outcome) or **confirmation bias** (seeking information that confirms negative beliefs). These biases cloud judgment and hinder our ability to solve problems effectively. Positivity, on the other hand, helps reduce these biases by encouraging a more balanced, optimistic view of the situation. This allows for clearer thinking and better decision-making.

c) **Resourcefulness and Adaptability**: Positive thinkers are more resourceful and adaptable. They believe that they have the ability to find solutions, even in challenging circumstances. This mindset fosters adaptability, as they are willing to explore new approaches and think outside the box. Their belief in their ability to overcome obstacles fuels their resourcefulness, helping them navigate complex problems with greater ease.

Real-Life Examples of People Who Transformed Their Lives by Changing Their Mindset

The power of a positive mindset is not just theoretical—it has transformed the lives of countless individuals across various fields. Here are a few real-life examples of people who embraced positivity and changed their lives for the better:

1. **Oprah Winfrey**: Oprah's journey from a difficult childhood marked by poverty and abuse to becoming one of the most influential media moguls in the world is a testament to the power of positive thinking. Oprah has often spoken about how her belief in herself and her unwavering optimism helped her rise above her circumstances. Despite facing numerous setbacks early in her career, she maintained a positive mindset, viewing every challenge as an opportunity to learn and grow. Today, Oprah's story inspires millions, showcasing how positivity can fuel success and transformation.

2. **J.K. Rowling**: Before becoming the best-selling author of the Harry Potter series, J.K. Rowling faced numerous personal and professional struggles, including unemployment, divorce, and rejection from multiple publishers. However, Rowling's positive mindset kept her

moving forward. She believed in the value of her work and persevered through rejections, eventually achieving global success. Her story is a powerful example of how positivity, combined with resilience, can lead to extraordinary achievements.

3. **Nelson Mandela**: Nelson Mandela's life exemplifies the transformative power of a positive mindset. Despite spending 27 years in prison during South Africa's apartheid era, Mandela maintained an optimistic outlook, believing in the possibility of a better future for his country. His unwavering positivity and belief in reconciliation and peace helped him lead South Africa out of apartheid and into a new era of democracy. Mandela's ability to stay positive in the face of immense hardship inspired millions and remains a powerful example of how positivity can change the world.

Evidence-Based Research Supporting the Power of Positivity

The benefits of positivity are not just anecdotal—they are supported by a growing body of scientific research. Here are some key studies that highlight the power of positivity:

1. **Barbara Fredrickson's Broaden-and-Build Theory**: Psychologist Barbara Fredrickson developed the *broaden-and-build theory* of positive emotions, which suggests that positive emotions broaden our cognitive abilities and help us build lasting psychological resources. Her research found that positivity enhances our ability to think creatively, solve problems, and build social connections, which are critical for personal and professional success.

2. **Positive Psychology Interventions**: Research in the field of positive psychology has shown that interventions aimed at increasing positive thinking—such as gratitude journaling, practicing mindfulness, and focusing on strengths—can lead to significant improvements in mental health and well-being. A meta-analysis of positive psychology interventions published in *The Journal of Positive Psychology* found that these practices lead to increased happiness, reduced depression, and greater life satisfaction.

3. **Optimism and Health**: A study published in the journal *Circulation* found that individuals with an optimistic outlook

were significantly less likely to experience heart disease and other cardiovascular issues compared to pessimists. The researchers concluded that positivity promotes better heart health by reducing stress, promoting healthier behaviours, and improving immune function.

The benefits of a positive mindset are vast and far-reaching, impacting everything from our physical health to our personal success and relationships. Positivity empowers us to face challenges with resilience, approach problems with creativity, and build stronger, more fulfilling connections with others. Supported by scientific research and real-life examples, the power of positivity is clear: it's a transformative force that can improve our lives in profound ways. By cultivating a positive mindset, we open the door to greater well-being, success, and happiness

10 Easy Everyday Tips to Increase Positive Thinking

Incorporating positive thinking into your daily routine is easier than you might think. While major life changes can help transform your mindset, small, consistent actions taken each day can make a significant impact. In this guide, I'll break down 10 easy and practical tips to boost your positivity, each grounded in science and proven strategies. These techniques are simple, but when practiced regularly, they can shift your thinking and bring more joy, optimism, and resilience into your life.

1. Practice Gratitude

Gratitude is one of the most powerful tools for cultivating positivity. By focusing on the things you're grateful for, you shift your attention away from what's lacking or going wrong and towards what's abundant in your life.

How to implement it: Start by keeping a gratitude journal. Each day, write down three to five things you're thankful for, whether big or small. It could be as simple as enjoying a nice cup of coffee in the morning or appreciating a meaningful conversation with a friend.

Why it works: Gratitude rewires your brain. Studies show that practicing gratitude can enhance mental health, boost happiness, and reduce symptoms of depression. According to research from the University of California, gratitude practices stimulate the production of dopamine and serotonin—neurotransmitters that play a key role in emotional well-being.

Shifting Mindsets

Key takeaway: Focusing on gratitude helps you become more aware of the positives in your life. Over time, it builds an optimistic mindset, as you begin to see the silver linings in even the most challenging situations.

2. Reframe Negative Thoughts

One of the core aspects of positive thinking is how you interpret challenges. Reframing negative thoughts doesn't mean ignoring problems but rather choosing to view them from a constructive perspective.

How to implement it: When you catch yourself thinking negatively, pause and challenge the thought. Ask yourself questions like: *Is there another way to see this situation? What can I learn from this? Is this thought fact-based, or is it an exaggerated worry?*

For example, instead of thinking, "I'm terrible at this task," reframe it to "I'm still learning, and every challenge is an opportunity to improve."

Why it works: According to cognitive-behavioural therapy (CBT), how we perceive events affects our emotional and behavioural responses. When you actively reframe negative thoughts, you interrupt the cycle of negativity and shift towards more rational and positive perspectives. Research in psychology shows that people who can reframe stressors are more resilient and experience less anxiety.

Key takeaway: By changing how you interpret situations, you take control of your mindset and reduce the power that negative thinking has over your life.

3. Surround Yourself with Positive Influences

The people you spend time with significantly impact your thinking. Surrounding yourself with positive influences can reinforce an optimistic mindset.

How to implement it: Take a look at your social circles. Are the people around you generally uplifting, or do they tend to focus on negativity? Make a conscious effort to spend more time with individuals who inspire, support, and encourage you. Join groups or communities focused on growth and positivity, whether it's through hobbies, personal development, or online communities.

Why it works: Studies on social contagion show that emotions are contagious. When you're around positive, motivated individuals, their mindset naturally influences your own. Conversely, negative environments can pull you down emotionally. A Harvard study

Shifting Mindsets

found that happiness spreads through social networks, and being around happy people increases your own happiness by as much as 25%.

Key takeaway: Who you surround yourself with matters. Choose your company wisely, and make sure the people in your life uplift and support your journey toward positivity.

4. Visualize Your Success

Visualization is a powerful technique used by athletes, business leaders, and high achievers to boost confidence and create a positive mindset.

How to implement it: Spend a few minutes each day visualizing yourself succeeding. Close your eyes and imagine what it looks and feels like to achieve your goals, whether they're personal or professional. Be specific—visualize the steps you'll take, the feelings you'll experience, and the positive outcomes of your efforts.

Why it works: Visualization works by training your brain to recognize success. Neuroscience research has found that the brain doesn't differentiate much between real and imagined experiences. By visualizing positive outcomes, you prime your mind to expect success, which boosts motivation and confidence. According to a study published in *The Journal of Consulting Psychology*, visualization techniques significantly improve performance and problem-solving abilities.

Key takeaway: By regularly visualizing success, you program your brain to believe in positive outcomes, which increases the likelihood of achieving them.

5. Focus on Solutions, Not Problems

When challenges arise, it's easy to get bogged down in problems. But solution-focused thinking can shift your mindset and help you stay positive, even in difficult situations.

How to implement it: When faced with a problem, instead of fixating on what went wrong, ask yourself, *What's the solution?* or *How can I improve this situation?* Shifting your focus from the issue itself to the possible ways forward fosters positivity and action.

Why it works: Solution-focused thinking aligns with the growth mindset, which emphasizes learning and adaptability. Instead of feeling stuck, this approach encourages problem-solving and creativity. Studies show that focusing on solutions enhances cognitive flexibility, which is crucial for overcoming obstacles and reducing stress.

Key takeaway: The next time you're faced with a challenge, turn your attention to potential solutions. This shift in focus will keep you moving forward with a positive outlook, no matter the obstacle.

6. Practice Self-Compassion

Being kind to yourself is essential for fostering positivity. Self-compassion means treating yourself with the same kindness and understanding that you would offer a close friend.

How to implement it: When you make a mistake or face a setback, avoid harsh self-criticism. Instead, acknowledge your feelings, remind yourself that setbacks are part of the human experience, and treat yourself with patience and kindness. A simple self-compassion exercise is to place your hand on your heart and silently offer yourself words of comfort and encouragement.

Why it works: Self-compassion reduces negative self-talk and fosters emotional resilience. Research by Dr. Kristin Neff, a leading expert on self-compassion, shows that self-compassionate individuals experience lower levels of stress and anxiety and are more motivated to improve themselves than those who engage in harsh self-criticism.

Key takeaway: Cultivating self-compassion helps you maintain a positive outlook by treating yourself kindly, especially in challenging moments.

7. Set Positive Intentions for the Day

Starting your day with a positive intention can set the tone for how you approach challenges and interactions.

How to implement it: Each morning, take a moment to set a positive intention for the day. It could be as simple as, *Today, I will focus on finding joy in my work*, or *Today, I will approach challenges with curiosity rather than frustration*. Write it down or say it aloud to reinforce the intention in your mind.

Why it works: Setting intentions helps align your thoughts, actions, and emotions with your goals. A study in *The Journal of Positive Psychology* found that individuals who set daily positive intentions experienced increased focus, reduced stress, and greater emotional regulation throughout the day.

Key takeaway: By setting a positive intention each morning, you direct your mindset toward positivity and become more mindful of your thoughts and actions throughout the day.

8. Engage in Mindful Breathing

Mindful breathing is a simple yet powerful tool for promoting calmness and positivity.

How to implement it: Throughout the day, take a few moments to focus on your breath. Close your eyes, inhale deeply through your nose, hold for a few seconds, and then slowly exhale through your mouth. As you breathe, let go of any negative thoughts or tension.

Why it works: Mindful breathing activates the parasympathetic nervous system, which promotes relaxation and reduces stress. A study published in *Frontiers in Psychology* found that mindful breathing enhances emotional regulation and increases positive emotions, leading to greater overall well-being.

Key takeaway: Incorporating mindful breathing into your day helps you stay grounded and calm, reducing stress and fostering a positive mindset.

9. Celebrate Small Wins

Celebrating small achievements, no matter how minor, helps reinforce a positive mindset and builds momentum toward larger goals.

How to implement it: At the end of each day, reflect on your accomplishments—big or small. Did you complete a task you've been putting off? Did you take a step toward a larger goal? Acknowledge and celebrate these moments. Write them down in a journal or share them with a friend.

Why it works: Celebrating small wins triggers the brain's reward system, releasing dopamine, which enhances motivation and happiness. According to a study published in *Harvard Business Review*, recognizing small achievements leads to a greater sense of progress and boosts long-term success.

Key takeaway: By celebrating small wins, you create a positive feedback loop that motivates and encourages further progress.

10. Limit Negative Media Consumption

While staying informed is important, constant exposure to negative news can skew your worldview and diminish positivity.

How to implement it: Be mindful of how much time you spend consuming negative news or media. Limit your news intake to specific times of the day, and balance it by seeking out positive stories, inspirational content, or educational material that uplifts and informs.

Why it works: Research shows that prolonged exposure to negative news can increase anxiety, stress, and pessimism. A study published in *The British Journal of Psychology* found that people who

Shifting Mindsets

reduced their consumption of negative media experienced improved mental health and greater optimism.

Key takeaway: Balancing your media consumption with positive, inspiring content helps you maintain a more optimistic and positive outlook on life.

# CHAPTER 3: SELF-AWARENESS AS THE FIRST STEP

The Self-awareness is the foundation of personal growth and transformation. To change your mindset and develop a more positive outlook, the first step is understanding where you currently stand. By becoming more aware of your thoughts, behaviours, and triggers, you can start to identify patterns that may be holding you back. In this chapter, we'll explore how to cultivate self-awareness, recognize negative thought patterns, and take actionable steps to move past limiting beliefs.

1. How to Identify Your Current Mindset: Recognizing Negative Patterns

The first step in becoming self-aware is recognizing the mindset you currently operate within. Most people go through life on autopilot, unaware of the thoughts and beliefs driving their behaviours. If you don't know what your mindset is, it's hard to change it. Understanding whether your mindset is primarily fixed or growth-oriented can reveal whether you're viewing challenges as opportunities for growth or as obstacles you can't overcome.

What is a Fixed vs. Growth Mindset?

Psychologist Carol Dweck coined the terms "fixed mindset" and "growth mindset" to describe how people approach learning and personal development. Those with a fixed mindset believe their talents and intelligence are static traits. They may avoid challenges, feel threatened by others' success, or give up easily when faced with adversity. On the other hand, those with a growth mindset believe they can develop their abilities through effort, learning, and perseverance.

Signs of a fixed mindset include:
- Frequently using phrases like, "I can't," "I'm not good at this," or "It's just who I am."
- Avoiding challenges out of fear of failure.
- Focusing on proving your intelligence or ability rather than improving.
- Feeling jealous or threatened by others' success.

Signs of a growth mindset include:
- Embracing challenges as opportunities to learn.

- Believing effort leads to mastery.
- Viewing failure as a stepping stone to success.
- Being inspired by others' achievements.

How to become aware of your mindset: To begin recognizing your current mindset, start by observing your inner dialogue throughout the day. What do you say to yourself when you face challenges? How do you react when things don't go as planned? One practical method is to record your thoughts in a journal when you feel frustrated, stuck, or inadequate. Patterns will begin to emerge that show whether you are operating from a fixed or growth mindset.

Why it matters:
Your mindset influences every area of your life, from your career success to your relationships and personal growth. By identifying whether your default mode of thinking is more fixed or growth-oriented, you can begin making conscious changes. Recognizing a fixed mindset is the first step toward rewiring your brain for positivity and adaptability.

2. Exercises for Developing Self-Awareness (e.g., Journaling, Mindfulness)

Building self-awareness isn't a one-time exercise—it's an ongoing process. To deepen your understanding of your mindset and thought patterns, it's essential to practice tools that help you observe your inner world. Journaling and mindfulness are two powerful techniques that can help you increase self-awareness and gain clarity on your thoughts, emotions, and behaviours.

Journaling for Self-Reflection

Journaling is a simple yet effective way to observe your thoughts, explore your emotions, and track patterns over time. When you journal, you externalize your thoughts, which gives you a clearer perspective. This practice allows you to recognize negative thought patterns and limiting beliefs that might otherwise go unnoticed.

How to get started with journaling:
- **Set aside time each day**: Find a quiet space and commit to journaling for at least 10–15 minutes a day. Write freely without censoring yourself, focusing on your thoughts, feelings, and any challenges you've faced.
- **Use prompts to guide you:** If you're not sure where to start, try prompts such as: "What's been on my mind lately?" "What's one challenge I'm facing right now?" or "How did

Shifting Mindsets

I react to a difficult situation today?"
- **Review your entries**: As you journal consistently, go back and review previous entries to identify recurring themes. Do you notice any negative patterns in how you talk to yourself or respond to challenges? Are there situations that consistently trigger self-doubt or frustration?

Mindfulness for Present-Moment Awareness

Mindfulness is the practice of staying present in the moment without judgment. It helps you become more aware of your thoughts, emotions, and bodily sensations as they arise. Through mindfulness, you can develop a greater sense of self-awareness and catch negative thought patterns before they spiral out of control.

How to practice mindfulness:
- **Start with breathing exercises**: A simple way to begin is by focusing on your breath. Sit comfortably, close your eyes, and pay attention to the sensation of each inhale and exhale. When your mind wanders, gently bring your focus back to your breath. This practice helps you become more attuned to the present moment and less reactive to stressors.
- **Observe your thoughts**: During mindfulness meditation, you'll naturally notice thoughts arising. Instead of getting caught up in them, practice observing them as if you were an outsider. Are your thoughts primarily positive, neutral, or negative? Are you replaying past events or worrying about the future? This observation helps you become more aware of your mental habits.
- **Body scan meditation**: Another mindfulness exercise is the body scan, where you bring attention to different parts of your body, noticing any tension or discomfort. This practice helps you tune into how your emotions manifest physically and can bring awareness to stress or anxiety you might not have been consciously aware of.

Why these exercises work:

Both journaling and mindfulness help you slow down and tune into your internal world. These practices enable you to become more aware of your thoughts, feelings, and behaviours, providing insights into where negative patterns might be sabotaging your efforts to stay positive.

3. Understanding the Triggers of Negative Thinking

Once you become more aware of your thoughts and behaviours, the next step is understanding what triggers your negative thinking. Everyone has triggers—situations, people, or events that set off a cascade of negative thoughts and emotions. Recognizing these triggers is crucial because it allows you to manage your reactions and avoid falling into destructive thought patterns.

Common triggers of negative thinking:

- **Stressful situations**: High-pressure environments, deadlines, or overwhelming tasks can trigger stress and negative thinking.
- **Interpersonal conflict**: Arguments or tension in relationships can activate feelings of insecurity, guilt, or frustration.
- **Perfectionism**: The need to always get things "just right" can lead to self-criticism and anxiety, especially when things don't go as planned.
- **Past trauma or negative experiences**: Unresolved emotional wounds from the past can resurface in present-day situations, triggering negative thinking.
- **Social comparison**: Comparing yourself to others, especially on social media, can lead to feelings of inadequacy, jealousy, and low self-esteem.

How to identify your triggers:

To better understand your triggers, pay attention to moments when your mood shifts from positive to negative. Notice what's happening in your environment when you start feeling anxious, angry, or down. Keeping a trigger journal can help. Each time you notice a shift in your mood, write down what happened just before, how it made you feel, and what thoughts arose in response.

For example, if you feel upset after seeing someone's vacation photos on social media, write down the situation (scrolling through Instagram), the emotion (jealousy or inadequacy), and the thought pattern ("I'll never be able to afford something like that"). Over time, you'll notice patterns in what triggers your negative thinking.

Why it matters:

Understanding your triggers empowers you to take control of your emotional responses. Instead of being blindsided by negativity, you can anticipate potential triggers and develop healthier coping mechanisms. You'll also begin to see that many triggers are external, and you have the power to choose how you react to them.

4. How to Accept and Move Past Limiting Beliefs

Limiting beliefs are deeply ingrained thoughts that hold you back from reaching your full potential. These beliefs often develop during childhood or in response to challenging experiences, and they can create self-imposed barriers that prevent you from pursuing your goals or adopting a positive mindset. Learning to accept and move past limiting beliefs is a critical step in shifting your mindset toward growth and positivity.

What are limiting beliefs?
Limiting beliefs are false assumptions you make about yourself and your capabilities. They often manifest as "I can't" or "I'm not" statements, such as:
- "I'm not smart enough to achieve success."
- "I'm not good at public speaking, so I'll never be able to advance in my career."
- "I can't start my own business because I don't have the skills or experience."

These beliefs are usually not grounded in reality but rather in fear or past experiences that didn't go as planned. Over time, they become self-fulfilling prophecies—because you believe them, you unconsciously act in ways that reinforce them.

How to identify limiting beliefs:
Start by questioning the assumptions you make about yourself. When you encounter a situation that makes you feel inadequate or unworthy, ask yourself, *What belief is driving this feeling?* Write down the belief and challenge it with evidence. For instance, if your limiting belief is "I'm not good enough to get that promotion," ask yourself, *Is there any evidence to support this belief?* More often than not, you'll find that your belief is based on fear or self-doubt rather than fact.

How to move past limiting beliefs:
- **Challenge your beliefs**: Once you've identified a limiting belief, it's time to challenge it. Ask yourself questions like, *Is this belief true? What evidence do I have that contradicts this belief?* For example, if your belief is "I'm not good enough," think about past achievements or compliments you've received that disprove this thought.
- **Replace with empowering beliefs**: After you've

challenged a limiting belief, replace it with a more empowering one. Instead of saying, "I'm not good enough," replace it with, "I'm constantly growing and improving, and I have the ability to succeed."
- **Take action**: The final step in overcoming limiting beliefs is to take action. Even if your new belief feels uncomfortable at first, act as if it's true. If you've replaced "I can't start a business" with "I can learn the skills to start a business," begin taking steps toward that goal, such as signing up for a course or networking with entrepreneurs.

Why it matters:

Limiting beliefs are mental roadblocks that prevent you from living a full, positive life. By identifying and challenging them, you can free yourself from self-imposed limitations and step into a mindset of growth, possibility, and resilience. Self-awareness is the foundation of mindset transformation. By identifying your current mindset, developing self-awareness through journaling and mindfulness, understanding your triggers, and moving past limiting beliefs, you empower yourself to create lasting, positive change in your life. Self-awareness gives you the insight needed to break free from negativity and cultivate a mindset rooted in growth, optimism, and possibility.

CHAPTER 4: REWIRING THE BRAIN FOR POSITIVITY

Introduction to Neuroplasticity: How the Brain Can Change

The human brain is an incredibly powerful organ, capable of adapting, evolving, and transforming throughout a person's life. For years, scientists believed that the brain's structure and function were fixed after childhood, but ground-breaking research has shown otherwise. This ability to change is known as **neuroplasticity**—the brain's capacity to form and reorganize synaptic connections in response to learning, experience, or even injury.

In this chapter, we'll explore how you can harness the science of neuroplasticity to reshape your mindset, rewire negative thought patterns, and cultivate positivity in your daily life. This transformation isn't just theoretical; it's backed by decades of neuroscience research and supported by practical techniques that you can start using today.

What is Neuroplasticity?

Neuroplasticity refers to the brain's ability to change and adapt its structure and function in response to experiences, new learning, or environmental factors. Essentially, neuroplasticity is what allows the brain to form new neural connections, strengthen existing ones, and reorganize itself based on how it's used. This ability is fundamental to personal development and healing because it means that, regardless of age or previous experiences, we can alter our brain's wiring to think more positively and develop healthier mental habits.

The Two Types of Neuroplasticity

1. **Structural Plasticity**: This refers to the brain's ability to physically change its structure. Neurons can form new connections or strengthen existing ones, making certain thought patterns or behaviours more dominant over time. For example, when you practice positive thinking consistently, the neural pathways associated with optimism become stronger, making it easier to adopt a positive outlook in the future.

2. **Functional Plasticity**: This is the brain's ability to shift functions from damaged areas to undamaged areas. Functional plasticity is particularly important in cases of

injury or trauma, but it also applies to emotional healing. For example, when someone learns to reframe negative experiences into positive lessons, their brain starts to rewire how it processes similar emotions in the future.

Why Neuroplasticity is Important for Positivity

Neuroplasticity is crucial for mindset transformation because it means that our thought patterns and behaviours aren't set in stone. Even deeply ingrained habits of negative thinking can be changed with intentional practice and focus. The more we engage in positive behaviours and thoughts, the stronger the neural connections supporting positivity become. This isn't just about thinking happy thoughts—it's about rewiring the brain to default to optimism, resilience, and growth, rather than negativity and fear.

How Negative Thought Patterns are Formed

Negative thought patterns often develop as a result of repeated experiences, trauma, or learned behaviours. If someone is exposed to negativity or stress for a prolonged period, the brain creates neural pathways that make negative thinking more automatic. Over time, these pathways become the brain's default response to challenges, making it harder to think positively without conscious effort.

For example, if a person frequently tells themselves, "I'm not good enough" or "I always fail," their brain strengthens those connections, making self-doubt and pessimism the go-to responses in difficult situations. However, neuroplasticity also means that these negative patterns can be unlearned and replaced with healthier, more optimistic ways of thinking.

Practical Techniques for Rewiring Negative Thought Patterns

Neuroplasticity offers the possibility of changing deeply ingrained thought patterns, but it requires consistent effort and practice. Below are four powerful techniques backed by research that can help you rewire your brain for positivity?

Affirmations

Affirmations are simple yet powerful statements that reinforce positive beliefs about yourself, your abilities, and your potential. When used consistently, affirmations help to reprogram the subconscious mind and cultivate a more positive and resilient outlook on life. The science behind affirmations lies in repetition—by frequently repeating positive statements, you reinforce neural pathways that support optimism and confidence.

How Affirmations Work in the Brain

When you repeat a positive statement, even if you don't fully believe it at first, you activate certain neural circuits in the brain. Over time, as these circuits are activated repeatedly, they become stronger, making the belief more ingrained. For example, if you constantly tell yourself, "I am capable of handling anything that comes my way," your brain starts to accept that as a default belief. This repetition helps create new neural pathways that make the belief stronger and more automatic over time.

How to Use Affirmations Effectively

- **Be specific**: Instead of general statements like "I am happy," focus on specific areas where you want to see change. For example, "I am confident in my ability to handle challenges at work" is a more targeted affirmation.
- **Use the present tense**: Speak as though the desired outcome is already true. This helps train your brain to accept the affirmation as a reality. For example, instead of saying, "I will be successful," say, "I am successful in all that I do."
- **Repeat them daily**: Consistency is key to rewiring your brain. Make affirmations part of your daily routine, whether in the morning, before bed, or during moments of stress.
- **Believe in them**: It's important to attach emotion and belief to your affirmations. Even if it feels awkward at first, try to visualize yourself embodying the affirmation.

Visualization

Visualization is a mental technique where you imagine yourself successfully achieving a goal or embodying a certain mindset. This practice leverages the brain's neuroplasticity by creating mental images that the brain interprets as real experiences. Research shows that the brain doesn't always distinguish between a vividly imagined event and a real one, meaning that visualization can help prime the brain for positive outcomes.

How Visualization Affects the Brain

When you visualize a specific scenario, such as giving a successful presentation or achieving a personal goal, the brain activates many of the same neural circuits as if the event were actually happening. This creates a sense of familiarity and confidence when you encounter similar situations in real life. Visualization essentially trains your brain for success by rehearsing the desired outcome over and over, reinforcing the neural pathways associated with that positive experience.

How to Practice Effective Visualization
- **Get specific**: The more detailed your mental image, the more effective the visualization. Imagine not only what you'll achieve, but how you'll feel, what you'll see, and who will be involved.
- **Incorporate all senses**: Engage as many senses as possible in your visualization to make the experience feel more real. Picture the sights, sounds, and emotions of the moment.
- **Visualize regularly**: Like affirmations, visualization works best when practiced consistently. Spend a few minutes each day visualizing your goals or ideal mindset.
- **Use visualization to overcome challenges**: Don't just visualize success—also imagine yourself handling setbacks with grace and resilience. This helps prepare your brain to stay positive in the face of adversity.

Gratitude Journaling

Gratitude journaling is a practice where you regularly write down things you're thankful for. This simple habit has profound effects on mental well-being and positivity. Numerous studies have shown that practicing gratitude can improve mood, reduce stress, and increase overall life satisfaction. The act of focusing on positive aspects of life rewires the brain to look for more of the good, rather than dwelling on the bad.

How Gratitude Changes the Brain

When you consciously focus on things you're grateful for, the brain's reward centres are activated, releasing dopamine and serotonin, the "feel-good" chemicals. Over time, practicing gratitude strengthens these neural pathways, making it easier to experience positive emotions more frequently. In essence, gratitude helps shift your brain's focus from what's lacking to what's abundant in your life.

How to Start a Gratitude Journal
- **Set aside time each day**: Ideally, write in your gratitude journal either in the morning or before bed. This helps you start or end the day on a positive note.
- **Be specific**: Instead of writing generic statements like "I'm grateful for my family," get specific about what you

appreciate. For example, "I'm grateful for the conversation I had with my sister today."
- **Focus on small things**: Gratitude isn't only about the big moments in life. Train your brain to recognize small joys, like a good cup of coffee, a kind word from a colleague, or a beautiful sunset.
- **Review your journal regularly**: Reflecting on your past entries can help reinforce the habit of gratitude and remind you of the positive things you've experienced.

Positive Self-Talk

Positive self-talk involves consciously replacing negative, self-defeating thoughts with more constructive and affirming ones. This mental shift can have profound effects on confidence, resilience, and overall mental health. Like affirmations, positive self-talk rewires the brain's thought patterns, helping to create a default mode of optimism and self-empowerment.

The Science behind Positive Self-Talk

When you engage in positive self-talk, your brain forms new neural pathways that reinforce feelings of self-worth and capability. Studies show that people who practice positive self-talk are more likely to be resilient in the face of challenges and maintain a hopeful outlook, even in difficult situations. This mental habit not only enhances mood but also improves performance in areas like sports, work, and relationships.

How to Practice Positive Self-Talk

- **Catch negative thoughts**: The first step is becoming aware of when you're engaging in negative self-talk. Pay attention to moments of doubt, fear, or self-criticism.
- **Reframe the thought**: Once you recognize a negative thought, challenge it by asking yourself if it's really true. Then, replace it with a more positive or realistic statement. For example, instead of "I always mess things up," say, "I've learned from past mistakes, and I'm getting better every day."
- **Be consistent**: Like any habit, positive self-talk takes time and repetition. Make it a daily practice, especially during moments of stress or uncertainty.

Daily Habits to Reinforce Positive Thinking

Rewiring your brain for positivity isn't something that happens overnight. It requires consistent practice and the development of daily habits that support a positive mindset. Below are some habits that can help you cultivate and maintain positivity over the long term.

Morning Routines

How you start your day sets the tone for the rest of it. Incorporating positive practices into your morning routine can help prime your brain for positivity and resilience throughout the day.

Mindful Breaks

Taking short, mindful breaks throughout your day helps reset your mind, reduces stress, and reinforces positive thinking. Mindfulness practices like deep breathing, meditation, or a brief walk in nature can help ground you in the present moment and reduce anxiety.

Nightly Reflections

Ending your day with a reflection on positive moments helps solidify those memories and strengthens the neural pathways associated with positivity. Before bed, write down three things that went well that day, or mentally review the highlights.

Building Mental Resilience to Overcome Setbacks

No matter how positive you become, life will still present challenges. Mental resilience is the ability to bounce back from adversity and continue moving forward with optimism and strength. By cultivating resilience, you train your brain to remain positive even in the face of obstacles.

How Resilience Affects the Brain

Resilience strengthens the brain's ability to regulate emotions, manage stress, and maintain a positive outlook even in difficult times. Neuroplasticity allows the brain to adapt to stress, meaning that the more you practice resilience, the better equipped your brain becomes at handling future challenges.

Strategies for Building Resilience

- **Reframe challenges as opportunities**: When faced with a setback, ask yourself, "What can I learn from this?" or "How can this make me stronger?" This shifts your brain's focus from negativity to growth.
- **Stay connected**: Strong social support is crucial for resilience. Surround yourself with positive, supportive

people who encourage you during tough times.
- **Practice self-compassion**: Be kind to yourself when things don't go as planned. Treat yourself with the same compassion and understanding you would offer a friend.

Rewiring your brain for positivity is not only possible, but it's a scientifically proven process that anyone can achieve with dedication and practice. Through techniques like affirmations, visualization, gratitude journaling, and positive self-talk, you can reshape your neural pathways to default to optimism and resilience. By incorporating daily habits and building mental resilience, you create a foundation for lasting positivity that will support your personal growth, mental health, and overall well-being.

10 Tips for Preparing to Leave a Long-Term Job and Starting Your Own Business

Tip 1: Clarify Your Vision

Before taking the leap from your long-term job, it's essential to have a clear vision for your business. Start by asking yourself what you truly want to achieve. What's the purpose of your business? What kind of lifestyle do you want to lead as an entrepreneur? A clear vision gives you a sense of direction and keeps you grounded when challenges arise. It also serves as a reminder of why you're making this big change in the first place.

Take time to write down your goals and the impact you want your business to have. Whether you aim to create a lifestyle of freedom, build a legacy, or make a difference in your industry, your vision is your North Star. Break it down into short-term and long-term goals so you can visualize your progress over time.

Being specific will also help you align your daily actions with your broader vision, keeping you focused when distractions or doubts try to creep in. When your purpose is clear, every decision you make, every step you take, will feel more intentional, and that clarity can build unshakable confidence.

Tip 2: Build a Financial Safety Net

One of the biggest concerns when leaving a stable job is financial uncertainty. Before making the transition, it's crucial to establish a safety net. This gives you the freedom to focus on growing your business without the constant worry of running out of funds. Ideally, aim to save at least six months to a year's worth of living expenses.

Additionally, calculate how much you'll need to start your

business. Do thorough research on startup costs, marketing expenses, and any other financial commitments. Understanding your financial needs early will prevent surprises down the road.

Think of your savings as the cushion that will support you through the initial growing pains of entrepreneurship. It will also give you peace of mind to explore, take risks, and invest in the right areas for long-term success. Many new business owners face financial pressure too early, but with proper preparation, you can avoid this pitfall.

Tip 3: Create a Solid Exit Strategy
A well-thought-out exit strategy is vital to leaving your job on good terms while preparing your new business for success. Start by giving adequate notice at your job, following any guidelines your employer may have for transitioning out of the role. The goal is to maintain professionalism and leave with your reputation intact—you never know when you may need those connections or references in the future.

While still employed, organize a timeline that aligns your job exit with the launch of your business. This timeline should include wrapping up tasks at work, training replacements, and completing any projects you're committed to. A smooth exit from your job will reduce stress and leave you feeling positive about the process.

Also, think about how you'll use your remaining time at your job to gather any last bits of knowledge or connections that may serve you as an entrepreneur. Having an exit strategy ensures that you leave on your own terms and are fully prepared for the next phase of your journey.

Tip 4: Develop Entrepreneurial Skills
Transitioning from an employee mindset to an entrepreneurial one requires a shift in skills and thinking. As an entrepreneur, you'll be responsible for every aspect of your business, from finances to marketing to customer service. Before leaving your job, invest time in developing these critical skills.

Start by identifying gaps in your knowledge or areas where you feel less confident. Take courses, read books, or even find a mentor who has successfully transitioned into business ownership. Key areas to focus on include time management, leadership, marketing, and financial planning.

The beauty of entrepreneurship is that you don't need to master everything right away, but being proactive about developing your skills will set you up for smoother growth. As you gain confidence in your abilities, you'll feel more empowered to tackle the challenges of starting your own business.

Tip 5: Build a Support System

Going from a structured job environment to running your own business can feel isolating at times. That's why building a strong support system is essential. Surround yourself with people who understand your goals and encourage your growth. This can include family, friends, mentors, or a network of like-minded entrepreneurs.

Join local or online communities where business owners share experiences, offer advice, and provide encouragement. The entrepreneurial journey has its ups and downs, and having a support system can make the tough days easier to navigate.

Find a mentor who has successfully made the leap from a traditional job to entrepreneurship. Their guidance can save you time and help you avoid common pitfalls. Having someone in your corner who's been through it all can give you confidence when doubt arises.

Tip 6: Test the Waters before the Big Leap

If possible, test your business idea while still working your full-time job. This could involve taking on freelance projects, offering your services to a small group of clients, or starting a side business. By doing so, you can gather feedback, tweak your approach, and make improvements before fully diving into entrepreneurship.

Testing the waters allows you to build momentum and validate your business idea without the full pressure of needing it to succeed immediately. You'll also gain insights into how much time, energy, and resources are required to make your business successful.

Once you start seeing results and gaining confidence in your business model, you'll feel more prepared to make the leap. Having some experience and proof of concept under your belt can make the transition much smoother.

Tip 7: Master Time Management

When you leave your job to start your own business, you gain the freedom to set your schedule. However, this freedom can also become a trap if you don't manage your time effectively. Successful entrepreneurs know how to structure their day for maximum productivity and focus.

Develop a routine that aligns with your natural energy levels. Prioritize tasks that directly contribute to the growth of your business, such as client acquisition, marketing, and product

Shifting Mindsets

development. Break your goals down into actionable steps and set deadlines to keep yourself accountable.

Remember that building a business takes time, so give yourself grace while staying committed to your schedule. Time management is key to avoiding burnout and ensuring steady progress toward your goals.

Tip 8: Focus on Building Relationships, Not Just Sales

When you start your own business, especially in the beginning stages, it's easy to become hyper-focused on sales. However, a key to long-term success is relationship building. Focus on creating genuine connections with your clients, customers, and community.

People want to do business with those they trust and feel connected to. Take the time to listen to your audience, understand their needs, and provide value beyond just a product or service. This approach will not only help you build a loyal customer base but also foster partnerships and opportunities that can grow your business.

Building relationships requires patience, but it's an investment that pays off in the long run. Strong relationships lead to repeat business, referrals, and a solid reputation in your industry.

Tip 9: Embrace the Power of Adaptability

Running your own business comes with uncertainties and challenges, but adaptability is one of the most important traits you can cultivate. Plans will change, obstacles will arise, and market conditions may shift. How you respond to these changes will determine your success as an entrepreneur.

Embrace flexibility and be open to new ideas and approaches. Rather than seeing setbacks as failures, view them as opportunities to learn and improve. The ability to pivot when necessary is a crucial skill that can make the difference between success and failure.

Adaptability also means staying curious and continually learning about your industry, market trends, and customer preferences. This mindset will help you stay ahead of the curve and seize new opportunities as they arise.

Tip 10: Celebrate Every Win, Big or Small

Starting your own business is a journey, and it's important to celebrate every step of the way. Whether you've signed your first client, launched your website, or completed your first month as an entrepreneur, take the time to acknowledge your progress.

Celebrating wins, no matter how small, reinforces a positive mindset and keeps you motivated for the next milestone.

Shifting Mindsets

Entrepreneurship can be a long road, and staying positive and optimistic is key to enduring through challenges. Reward yourself for your hard work and reflect on how far you've come.

By celebrating your progress, you're also fostering a mindset of gratitude and positivity, which will help you stay resilient and energized throughout your entrepreneurial journey. These ten tips will help you confidently transition from your long-term job into entrepreneurship, ensuring that you are prepared mentally, emotionally, and financially for the journey ahead. With the right mindset and support, you can make the leap and thrive in your new business.

CHAPTER 5: CULTIVATING OPTIMISM IN DAILY LIFE

Introduction: The Power of Optimism

The Optimism isn't just a fleeting emotion; it's a way of seeing the world that shapes every aspect of your life. Research shows that an optimistic mindset can boost mental and physical health, enhance relationships, and improve overall life satisfaction. It's the fuel behind perseverance and resilience, helping people find solutions rather than dwelling on problems.

In this chapter, we'll dive deep into how you can cultivate optimism in your daily life, no matter your circumstances. Whether you're dealing with everyday stress, facing big challenges, or simply looking to elevate your mindset, adopting a positive outlook can transform your experiences. You'll learn powerful strategies to shift your thinking, see the hidden opportunities in adversity, and reduce the anxieties that hold you back.

Strategies to Adopt a Positive Outlook in Everyday Situations

Adopting a positive outlook doesn't happen by accident; it's a practice that requires consistent effort, especially when life throws challenge your way. The good news is that optimism can be learned and strengthened like any other skill. By practicing specific strategies, you can shift your perspective and rewire your brain to focus on the brighter side of life.

1. Practice Gratitude Daily

Gratitude is one of the simplest and most effective ways to nurture optimism. When you actively focus on what you're thankful for, your brain starts to recognize more and more positive aspects of your day-to-day life. You stop taking the good things for granted and begin to see how much you already have.

Start by creating a daily gratitude practice. Each morning or evening, write down three things you're grateful for, no matter how big or small. It could be the support of a loved one, the warmth of the sun, or the accomplishment of a small task. Over time, this habit will shift your focus away from what's lacking in your life to the abundance around you.

Studies show that practicing gratitude can improve mood,

increase life satisfaction, and even enhance physical health. By consistently acknowledging the positives, you'll train your brain to automatically gravitate toward optimism.

2. Surround Yourself with Positivity
The people and environment you surround yourself with have a significant impact on your mindset. It's much easier to stay optimistic when you're around others who uplift, support, and encourage you. On the flip side, spending time with negative or cynical individuals can drain your energy and reinforce pessimistic thinking.

Take inventory of your social circle and ask yourself: Do the people around me help me grow? Do they inspire me to see possibilities, or do they focus on the negatives? You don't have to cut ties with everyone, but consciously choose to spend more time with those who add positivity to your life.

In addition to people, consider your environment. Is your space cluttered and stressful, or does it reflect peace and optimism? Small changes, like adding inspirational quotes, de-cluttering, or bringing in more natural light, can enhance your mood and outlook.

3. Use Affirmations to Shift Your Mindset
Affirmations are powerful, positive statements that you repeat to yourself to reprogram your subconscious mind. When you consistently affirm a positive belief, your brain starts to accept it as truth. Over time, this can create a significant shift in your self-perception and outlook on life.

Write down a few affirmations that resonate with you, such as "I am capable of overcoming any challenge," "Good things are coming my way," or "I choose to see the beauty in every situation." Repeat these affirmations throughout the day, especially during moments of doubt or negativity.

By aligning your thoughts with positive beliefs, you'll naturally start to see opportunities and solutions rather than obstacles.

Learning to Find Opportunity in Challenges
Optimism doesn't mean ignoring challenges or pretending that everything is perfect. It's about choosing to see obstacles as opportunities for growth and learning, rather than as roadblocks. When faced with difficulties, you have a choice: either dwell on the problem or look for the lesson within it. Learning to shift your focus in this way is a hallmark of resilient, optimistic people.

Shifting Mindsets

1. Reframe Setbacks as Stepping Stones

Everyone faces setbacks at some point, but what separates optimistic people from the rest is how they view these setbacks. Instead of seeing failure as the end, they view it as part of the journey toward success.

When you encounter a setback, ask yourself: What can I learn from this? How can this experience make me better or stronger? This simple shift in perspective allows you to see the value in adversity. Each challenge you overcome builds your confidence and resilience, preparing you for future success.

History is full of stories of people who turned their challenges into stepping stones. Thomas Edison, for example, famously failed thousands of times before successfully inventing the light bulb. But each failure taught him what didn't work, bringing him closer to his breakthrough.

2. Adopt a Growth Mindset

At the heart of finding opportunity in challenges is the concept of a growth mindset, developed by psychologist Carol Dweck. A growth mindset is the belief that your abilities and intelligence can be developed through effort, learning, and perseverance. In contrast, a fixed mindset leads you to believe that your abilities are static and unchangeable.

When you adopt a growth mindset, you view challenges as opportunities to grow rather than as tests of your innate abilities. This makes you more open to taking risks, learning from failures, and continuously improving.

To cultivate a growth mindset, start embracing challenges as opportunities to stretch your capabilities. Remind yourself that effort and persistence are what lead to success, not innate talent or intelligence. By focusing on growth, you'll naturally start to see the silver lining in difficult situations.

The Power of Reframing Negative Thoughts

Reframing is a cognitive technique that involves changing the way you interpret negative situations. Instead of automatically jumping to worst-case scenarios, reframing allows you to view challenges in a more constructive light. This doesn't mean denying reality—it means choosing a perspective that serves your well-being and empowers you to act.

Shifting Mindsets

1. Catch and Challenge Negative Thoughts
The first step in reframing is to become aware of your automatic negative thoughts. These are the thoughts that pop into your mind when things don't go as planned, such as "I'll never be able to do this" or "This always happens to me." These thoughts are often exaggerated or based on assumptions rather than facts.

Once you catch a negative thought, challenge it. Ask yourself: Is this really true? Is there another way to look at this situation? Often, you'll find that your negative thought is based on fear or a past experience rather than the present reality.

For example, if you're faced with a new challenge at work and your first thought is, "I'm going to fail," challenge that thought by reminding yourself of past successes or by considering how you can prepare to succeed. This shift in perspective allows you to approach the situation with more confidence and optimism.

2. Flip the Script
After challenging a negative thought, practice flipping the script by finding a positive or neutral way to interpret the situation. Instead of focusing on the potential for failure, think about what you can learn from the experience or how you can grow through the challenge.

For example, if you're facing a tight deadline at work and your initial thought is, "I'll never finish this on time," reframe it to, "This is an opportunity to practice my time-management skills and prove to myself that I can handle pressure." This shift in thinking helps reduce anxiety and boosts your motivation to take action.

The more you practice reframing, the more natural it becomes. Over time, you'll train your brain to automatically find the positive or constructive side of every situation.

Techniques to Stop Overthinking and Reduce Anxiety

Overthinking is a common barrier to optimism. When you overthink, you get stuck in a loop of analysing every possible outcome, which often leads to anxiety and inaction. The good news is that there are techniques you can use to quiet your mind and reduce overthinking, allowing you to approach life with more clarity and calm.

1. Practice Mindfulness
Mindfulness is the practice of staying present in the moment rather than getting lost in thoughts about the past or future. When you're mindful, you focus your attention on what's happening right now,

without judgment. This helps break the cycle of overthinking and brings you back to the present.

One simple mindfulness technique is to focus on your breath. Whenever you catch yourself overthinking, pause and take a few deep breaths. Focus on the sensation of the air entering and leaving your body. This helps calm your mind and brings you back to the present moment.

Mindfulness not only reduces overthinking but also helps you become more aware of your thoughts and emotions, allowing you to respond to situations with greater clarity and optimism.

2. Set Boundaries around Worry Time

If you find yourself constantly worrying about the future or overanalysing decisions, try setting boundaries around your worry time. Designate a specific time of day, such as 15 minutes in the evening, to focus on any concerns or decisions you need to make. During this time, write down your worries and possible solutions.

Once the time is up, close the notebook and move on with your day. This technique helps you compartmentalize your worries rather than letting them consume your entire day. It also gives you a sense of control over your thoughts, reducing the tendency to overthink.

3. Take Action to Break the Cycle

Overthinking often stems from indecision or fear of making the wrong choice. One of the best ways to break the cycle is to take action, even if it's a small step. Action brings clarity and reduces the mental clutter that comes with overanalysing.

When you find yourself stuck in overthinking, ask yourself: What's the smallest step I can take right now? It could be sending an email, making a phone call, or doing five minutes of research. Taking action shifts your focus from thinking to doing, which helps reduce anxiety and builds momentum.

Embracing Optimism as a Way of Life

Cultivating optimism in daily life is about more than just thinking happy thoughts; it's about choosing to see the world through a lens of possibility, growth, and resilience. By practicing gratitude, reframing negative thoughts, and finding opportunity in challenges, you can transform your mindset and, ultimately, your life. Optimism empowers you to navigate life's ups and downs with grace and confidence, knowing that every challenge is an opportunity for growth.

Shifting Mindsets

As you begin to adopt these practices, remember that optimism is a journey, not a destination. It requires consistent effort, but the rewards—improved well-being, stronger relationships, and a deeper sense of purpose are well worth it.

Key Skills of a Long-Serving Police Officer and How They Transition into Business

When transitioning from a long-term career in policing to entrepreneurship, there's an incredible skill set that police officers bring to the table, often without even realizing it. Years spent on the force provide invaluable tools that translate seamlessly into the world of business, offering distinct advantages in leadership, problem-solving, communication, and decision-making.

In this guide, we will explore some of the key skills developed as a police officer and how these can be leveraged effectively when starting your own business.

1. Leadership and Team Management

In Policing:

Leadership is a core element of any long-serving police officer's role. Officers are often responsible for leading teams during operations, managing the welfare of their colleagues, and making critical decisions that affect both the team and the community. Policing teaches officers how to lead under pressure, manage a diverse group of individuals, and inspire trust and respect among team members.

Transitioning to Business:

When starting your own business, leadership is key. Whether you're managing a small team or just yourself in the beginning, the ability to take charge, inspire others, and maintain focus under pressure is essential. Your experience in making quick, effective decisions in high-stress environments will give you the confidence to steer your business in the right direction, even during challenging times.

Additionally, a business owner must lead by example, setting the vision and culture for their company. The discipline, accountability, and ethical leadership developed as a police officer naturally transition into creating a values-driven business, which can foster a positive work environment and attract loyal employees.

2. Problem-Solving and Critical Thinking

In Policing:

Every day as a police officer presents new, often unpredictable problems that require quick thinking and effective solutions.

Shifting Mindsets

Officers are trained to assess situations rapidly, gather and interpret information, and respond with the best course of action. These critical thinking skills are honed through experience, whether it's handling a high-stakes situation on the streets or resolving internal conflicts within the department.

Transitioning to Business:
Entrepreneurship is, at its core, a series of problem-solving challenges. From navigating financial hurdles to solving customer needs, your ability to think critically and analytically will be one of your greatest assets. Business is unpredictable, much like policing, and your experience in handling unforeseen situations gives you a unique edge. Whether it's strategic planning, product development, or market positioning, your problem-solving mindset will allow you to pivot and adapt quickly.

Moreover, as a business owner, you'll often need to create innovative solutions to stay competitive. Your ability to think outside the box—developed on the job as an officer—will help you design creative strategies and stand out in a crowded market.

3. Effective Communication

In Policing:
Police officers must communicate clearly and effectively with a wide range of people—from colleagues and superiors to civilians in crisis situations. Officers learn how to remain calm and articulate in high-pressure environments, de-escalate conflicts, and build rapport with individuals from various backgrounds. Listening, empathy, and the ability to deliver information concisely are essential components of the job.

Transitioning to Business:
In business, communication is key. Whether you're negotiating with suppliers, presenting your business to investors, or building relationships with clients, clear and effective communication will be critical to your success. Your ability to remain calm and composed during difficult conversations will help you negotiate better deals and resolve conflicts swiftly.

Additionally, customer service is a cornerstone of any business. Your experience in de-escalation and handling difficult situations will enable you to manage customer relations effectively. Whether addressing complaints or providing support, your communication skills will set your business apart in terms of trust and reliability.

Shifting Mindsets

4. Time Management and Organizational Skills
In Policing:
Police officers must juggle multiple tasks simultaneously, whether it's managing paperwork, responding to incidents, or attending court proceedings. Time management is crucial, as is the ability to prioritize tasks effectively and stay organized in a demanding environment.

Transitioning to Business:
Running a business requires the same ability to prioritize and manage time. In the early stages of entrepreneurship, you may be wearing many hats—handling operations, marketing, finances, and customer service all at once. Your organizational skills, developed over years of managing cases, incidents, and reports, will help you maintain order in the chaos of building a business.

As an entrepreneur, there are constant demands on your time, and being able to focus on what's most important is essential. Setting clear goals, maintaining deadlines, and staying efficient will help keep your business on track.

5. Emotional Resilience and Stress Management
In Policing:
Police officers are exposed to high levels of stress and trauma, requiring emotional resilience and the ability to cope under pressure. Officers learn to manage their emotions, stay calm in crisis situations, and make clear-headed decisions even when faced with difficult circumstances.

Transitioning to Business:
Starting a business can be one of the most stressful endeavours, especially in the early stages when financial pressures, competition, and uncertainty are high. Your experience in handling stress and maintaining emotional control will give you an advantage as an entrepreneur. The resilience you've developed will help you push through challenging times, remain focused, and avoid burnout.

Building emotional resilience also allows you to maintain a balanced perspective, handling setbacks and failures with grace. In business, not everything will go according to plan, and being able to bounce back from disappointments and keep moving forward is key to long-term success.

6. Ethics and Integrity
In Policing:
Upholding the law requires a strong sense of ethics and integrity.

Police officers are trusted with significant responsibility, and they must act with honesty, fairness, and accountability in every aspect of their job. The values of integrity and ethical decision-making are deeply ingrained in the profession.

Transitioning to Business:
Integrity is a fundamental aspect of business success. Whether you're dealing with clients, employees, or partners, maintaining honesty and transparency will build trust and credibility. Customers are more likely to support a business that operates ethically, and long-term business relationships are built on the foundation of trust.

As a business owner, your reputation is everything. The ethical decision-making you've practiced throughout your police career will help you navigate the complexities of business while staying true to your values. This will not only set you apart from competitors but also create a brand that people respect and want to engage with.

7. Decision-Making under Pressure
In Policing:
Police officers are required to make quick, decisive judgments in high-stakes situations. Whether on a routine call or in a life-threatening scenario, they learn to gather relevant information, assess risks, and make decisions quickly, often with limited time and resources.

Transitioning to Business:
Entrepreneurs face similar pressure when it comes to decision-making, especially in fast-paced industries. Your ability to make informed decisions under pressure will be invaluable. In business, you often need to act swiftly to seize opportunities or pivot when challenges arise. Your experience in making tough calls will give you the confidence to trust your instincts and take calculated risks.

Additionally, your ability to weigh the consequences of different actions, learned on the job, will ensure that you make sound decisions that benefit your business in the long term.

8. Adaptability and Flexibility
In Policing:
The nature of police work is unpredictable. Officers need to be highly adaptable, responding to changing situations on the ground and adjusting their approach as new information comes in. Flexibility is a crucial trait, as no two days—or incidents—are ever the same.

Transitioning to Business:
The entrepreneurial landscape is constantly evolving, and being able

to adapt to new market trends, technologies, and customer needs is crucial. As an entrepreneur, you'll be faced with numerous changes, and your ability to stay flexible and pivot, when necessary, will keep your business relevant and competitive.

Your experience in quickly adapting to new situations as a police officer will help you navigate the ever-changing world of business, ensuring that you're always ready to seize opportunities and meet challenges head-on.

Leveraging Policing Skills for Entrepreneurial Success

Transitioning from a career in policing to entrepreneurship may seem like a significant shift, but the core skills you've developed as an officer are highly transferable and valuable in the business world. From leadership and decision-making to problem-solving and resilience, your experience equips you with a unique set of strengths that can set your business apart.

By recognizing and leveraging these skills, you can build a strong foundation for success as an entrepreneur. Your ability to handle pressure, think critically, and lead with integrity will not only help your business thrive but also make a positive impact on the lives of those you serve in your new venture.

How to Sell a Service Successfully: A Professional Guide to Success

Selling a service can be both an art and a science. Unlike selling physical products, which customers can hold, see, and directly assess, a service is intangible. Convincing potential clients of its value requires a blend of relationship-building, clear communication, and a deep understanding of your clients' needs. The challenge is to make the benefits of your service so compelling that customers feel confident in their investment.

In this guide, I'll Walk you through the steps to successfully sell a service, focusing on building trust, creating value, and turning prospects into long-term clients. We'll cover everything from positioning your service in the market to closing the deal, with actionable insights drawn from real-world experiences.

Step 1: Understand Your Target Market

Before you can effectively sell your service, it's crucial to understand your target market. Without knowing who your ideal customers are, what they value, and what challenges they face, your sales efforts will

be aimless.
- **Market Research:** Conduct thorough research to define your target audience. Consider demographic factors like age, gender, location, and income level, but go deeper into psychographics—what are their interests, pain points, and goals?
- **Identify Pain Points:** A pain point is a specific problem that your target audience faces and that your service solves. By understanding these challenges, you can tailor your service to meet their needs.
- **Customer Personas:** Develop detailed personas that represent the different segments of your target market. A persona should include the person's background, challenges, and motivations, allowing you to tailor your sales pitch for each type of client.

Understanding your audience not only helps in crafting the right message but also positions you as a solution to their specific problems, making your service more relevant and valuable in their eyes.

Step 2: Position Your Service with a Unique Value Proposition

Once you understand your target market, you need to clearly define what sets your service apart from competitors. This is where your **unique value proposition (UVP)** comes in.

- **Define Your UVP:** Your UVP should highlight what makes your service unique, how it solves your client's pain points, and why they should choose you over the competition. Be specific. For instance, if you offer web design services, your UVP might focus on the fact that you specialize in mobile-optimized, high-converting designs for small businesses.
- **Benefits, Not Features:** When crafting your UVP and sales pitch, focus on the benefits your service provides, rather than the features. For example, if you're selling a marketing consulting service, a feature might be "monthly reporting," but the benefit is "you'll get detailed insights that allow you to make informed decisions and increase your ROI."
- **Differentiation:** What makes your service stand out? Is it a special skill set, years of experience, or the customer service you provide? Highlight this difference consistently in your

sales messaging.

A strong value proposition shows potential clients exactly what they'll gain from your service and why they can't afford to go with anyone else.

Step 3: Develop a Clear Sales Process

A structured sales process is essential for converting leads into clients. Having a defined approach ensures that you're guiding prospects smoothly through each stage of the buying journey, from initial contact to closing the deal.

- **Lead Generation:** Start by identifying the channels through which you'll generate leads. This could be through content marketing, social media, networking events, or cold outreach. Ensure that you have a system for tracking these leads, whether it's a CRM system or a simple spreadsheet.
- **Qualify Your Leads:** Not every lead is a good fit for your service. It's important to quickly identify whether a potential client has the budget, authority, and need for your service. Asking the right questions early on can save you time and energy.
- **Sales Funnel:** Your sales funnel should outline each stage a potential client goes through, from awareness to decision. The key stages are:
    - **Awareness:** The prospect learns about your service.
    - **Interest:** They engage with your marketing materials, perhaps by visiting your website or downloading a free resource.
    - **Consideration:** They evaluate whether your service is the right fit.
    - **Decision:** They are ready to purchase.
    - **Post-Sale:** Retention and ongoing service.

By having a clear sales process, you can ensure that you're nurturing leads effectively and pushing them toward conversion without being too pushy or salesy.

Step 4: Create a Compelling Sales Presentation

Once you've generated leads and qualified them, the next step is to present your service in a way that is both engaging and persuasive. This is where your sales pitch comes in.

- **Know Your Audience:** Customize your presentation based on the needs and pain points of the specific prospect you're

addressing. Refer back to the customer personas and tailor the pitch accordingly.
- **Build Trust:** Trust is one of the most critical factors in service sales. Build it by showcasing your expertise, offering testimonials, case studies, and even a portfolio if applicable. Providing social proof demonstrates that your service has delivered results for others.
- **Engage Through Storytelling:** Rather than just listing facts about your service, engage your audience by telling a story. This could be the story of how your service helped a client achieve success, or even your personal journey and why you started offering this service.
- **Use Data:** Where possible, use data to back up your claims. If you offer marketing services, show potential clients specific metrics from previous campaigns (e.g., "We helped X client increase their sales by 30% in 6 months"). This gives your claims more credibility.

Step 5: Handle Objections with Empathy and Confidence

It's natural for potential clients to have objections during the sales process, but how you handle these objections can make or break the deal.

- **Common Objections:** Some common objections might include:
    - "The price is too high."
    - "I'm not sure this will work for me."
    - "I need to think about it."
- **Anticipate Objections:** The best way to handle objections is to anticipate them before they arise. For instance, if you know that cost is a common concern, be ready to explain the value behind your pricing. If you've done your homework on the client's needs, you can pre-emptively address any doubts.
- **Empathy and Listening:** When a client raise an objection, don't just jump into defines mode. Show empathy, listen carefully, and acknowledge their concern. For example, if a client says, "This seems too expensive," you might say, "I understand that budget is a concern, and I'd be happy to walk you through how our service saves money in the long run."
- **Confidence in Your Service:** Ultimately, handling

objections comes down to your confidence in your service. If you truly believe in the value you provide, this confidence will shine through in your responses, making it easier to persuade the client that your service is worth the investment.

Step 6: Close the Deal

After handling objections and delivering a solid presentation, the next step is closing the sale. Closing is about moving the client from the consideration phase to making a firm decision.

- **Create a Sense of Urgency:** Sometimes clients may delay making a decision. One way to close the sale is by creating a sense of urgency. You can offer limited-time discounts, highlight how taking action now will save them time or money, or even explain how waiting could lead to missed opportunities (e.g., "If we start now, you'll have everything ready for the holiday season").
- **Ask for the Sale:** Don't be afraid to ask for the sale. A soft close might involve asking, "Do you have any further questions before we get started?" or "Shall we get you booked in for next month?"
- **Contract and Next Steps:** Once the client agrees, make the process of on boarding seamless. Provide a contract or agreement that outlines the scope of services and next steps. Clear communication after the close ensures a smooth transition into the delivery phase.

Step 7: Deliver Exceptional Service to Retain Clients

The sale doesn't end when the client signs on the dotted line. Retaining clients and encouraging repeat business is crucial to the long-term success of your service-based business.

- **Deliver on Your Promise:** Ensure that the service you deliver matches or exceeds the expectations you set during the sales process. Consistency and quality are key to retaining clients.
- **Build Relationships:** Stay in touch with your clients and check in regularly. Building strong relationships can lead to repeat business and referrals. Send personalized emails or updates, provide value with insights, or offer exclusive services to loyal customers.
- **Request Feedback:** Asking for feedback after delivering your service shows that you're committed to improvement

and care about the client's experience. It's also an opportunity to gather testimonials and case studies, which you can use to attract new clients.

Step 8: Use Referrals to Grow Your Business

Word-of-mouth referrals can be one of the most effective ways to grow your service-based business.

- **Ask for Referrals:** Don't be shy about asking satisfied clients for referrals. You can say, "If you know anyone else who might benefit from our service, we'd greatly appreciate a recommendation."
- **Referral Incentives:** Offering a referral incentive, such as a discount or bonus for each new client a current customer brings in, can be a great motivator for your clients to spread the word.
- **Build a Referral Network:** Developing relationships with complementary businesses can also generate referrals. For instance, if you offer accounting services, partnering with a business coach might lead to mutual referrals.

Step 9: Measure Your Success and Adapt

The business landscape is always changing, so it's important to continuously measure your success and adapt your sales strategy as needed.

- **Track Key Metrics:** Monitor key performance indicators (KPIs) that reflect the health of your sales process. Common metrics to track include:
    - **Conversion Rate:** The percentage of leads that turn into paying clients.
    - **Customer Acquisition Cost (CAC):** The total cost of acquiring a new customer, including marketing and sales expenses.
    - **Customer Lifetime Value (CLV):** The total revenue you can expect from a client over the duration of your relationship.
    - **Client Retention Rate:** The percentage of clients who continue to use your service over time.

By analysing these metrics, you can gain insights into what's working and what needs improvement.

- **Solicit Feedback:** Regularly seek feedback from clients about their experience with your service and the sales process. Use surveys, one-on-one conversations, or follow-

up emails to gather their thoughts. This feedback can reveal areas for improvement, both in service delivery and sales tactics.
- **Adapt and Iterate:** The best sales strategies are not static; they evolve based on experience and market conditions. Be open to trying new approaches, experimenting with different messaging, or exploring new marketing channels. For example, if you find that social media leads are converting at a higher rate than email marketing, you might decide to allocate more resources toward social media.

Step 10: Continue Your Professional Development

The world of sales and marketing is ever-changing, so investing in your professional development is crucial to long-term success.

- **Attend Workshops and Seminars:** Look for local workshops, webinars, or conferences related to sales, marketing, and your specific industry. These events provide opportunities to learn from experts, network with peers, and gain fresh perspectives.
- **Read Industry Literature:** Keep up with the latest trends and best practices by reading books, articles, and blogs focused on sales and marketing. Subscribing to industry newsletters can also keep you informed about emerging strategies and tools.
- **Join Professional Groups:** Consider joining organizations or associations related to your field. These groups often offer valuable resources, training, and networking opportunities. Engaging with other professionals can also help you share experiences and learn from others' successes and challenges.

Successfully selling a service requires a comprehensive approach that encompasses understanding your market, crafting a compelling value proposition, and building relationships based on trust and transparency. Each step—from initial lead generation to closing the deal and retaining clients—is interconnected, and your success hinges on executing each phase effectively.

As you implement these strategies, remember that persistence and adaptability are key. The more you refine your approach and learn from each interaction, the better equipped you'll be to build a thriving service-based business.

By focusing on creating value for your clients, delivering

Shifting Mindsets

exceptional service, and continually measuring your success, you can foster long-term relationships and generate referrals that will support the sustainable growth of your business. With dedication and a positive mindset, you have the power to transform not only your own career but also the lives of your clients through the services you provide.

Additional Resources

To further support your journey in selling services successfully, consider exploring the following resources:

1. **Books:**
    - "The Challenger Sale" by Matthew Dixon and Brent Adamson
    - "Sell with a Story" by Paul Smith
    - "Never Split the Difference" by Chris Voss
2. **Online Courses:**
    - Coursera and Udemy offer courses on sales techniques and strategies.
    - HubSpot Academy provides free courses on inbound sales and marketing.
3. **Networking Groups:**
    - Local business chambers or online platforms like LinkedIn can help you connect with other professionals.

Remember, every great seller started where you are now. With the right strategies, mindset, and dedication, you too can master the art of selling services successfully.

CHAPTER 6. SURROUNDING YOURSELF WITH POSITIVITY

In the journey towards a positive mindset, we often overlook the importance of our environment and the people we surround ourselves with. Just as we cultivate a garden by ensuring it has the right soil, sunlight, and care, we need to cultivate our mental and emotional environment with the right influences to thrive. This chapter explores the profound impact that our surroundings—both physical and social—have on our mindset, and how we can consciously design our lives to be more positive, empowering, and growth-oriented.

How Your Environment and Social Circle Influence Your Mindset

We often hear the phrase, "You are the average of the five people you spend the most time with," and this statement holds a powerful truth. Human beings are inherently social creatures, shaped by the people and experiences we expose ourselves too daily. Whether we realize it or not, the mind constantly absorbs information from our surroundings, and this can either uplift or pull us down.

The Power of Environmental Cues

Your physical environment plays a significant role in shaping your emotions, thoughts, and overall mindset. A cluttered, chaotic space can often mirror a cluttered, chaotic mind. Conversely, a clean, organized, and aesthetically pleasing environment fosters clarity, focus, and peace. When you walk into a space that feels welcoming and orderly, your mind follows suit, becoming more open and receptive to positive thinking.

- **Physical Clutter and Mental Clarity**: Studies have shown that cluttered environments lead to higher levels of stress and distraction, making it harder to focus and think positively. By decluttering your home or workspace, you create mental space, making it easier to adopt a more positive outlook.
- **Personal Spaces as Reflection of Mindset**: Your home, office, or any personal space is a reflection of your inner world. If it's filled with negativity or elements that drain

your energy, you may subconsciously feel burdened. On the other hand, surrounding yourself with items that inspire and motivate you, such as vision boards, affirmations, or meaningful photographs, can trigger positive emotions and keep you aligned with your goals.
- **Lighting, Colours, and Energy**: Even the colours you surround yourself with can influence your mood. Warm, bright colours like yellow or orange can uplift your spirit, while cooler tones like blue or green can promote calm and relaxation. Lighting also plays a crucial role—natural light, for instance, has been shown to boost mood and energy levels, contributing to a more positive mindset.

Social Influence: The Energy of People around You

People are arguably the most significant element of your environment when it comes to shaping your mindset. The energy, beliefs, and attitudes of those around you are contagious. If you're surrounded by people who are constantly negative, cynical, or pessimistic, it can be incredibly challenging to maintain a positive outlook.

- **Emotional Contagion**: Research in psychology reveals that emotions are highly contagious. If your social circle is filled with individuals who are consistently complaining, doubting, or indulging in fear-based thinking, you're likely to absorb some of that negativity, even without realizing it. On the flip side, spending time with positive, growth-oriented individuals can uplift your spirit and reinforce your commitment to a positive mindset.
- **Feedback Loops**: Social feedback loops are cycles where our beliefs and behaviours are reinforced by the responses, we receive from those around us. If you're surrounded by people who consistently affirm your worth, support your dreams, and encourage your growth, you are far more likely to take positive actions and think positively about yourself. Conversely, if those around you doubt your abilities or discourage your aspirations, it can create a feedback loop that fosters self-doubt and negativity.

The Role of Community and Positive Relationships in Sustaining Positivity

We are wired for connection, and positive relationships serve as the backbone of mental and emotional well-being. Having a community that supports and uplifts you can be a crucial factor in sustaining a positive mindset, especially during challenging times. The right community acts as a buffer against stress and negativity, providing you with encouragement, advice, and love when you need it most.

Why Positive Relationships Matter

- **Emotional Support**: A network of caring, positive individuals provides emotional support during tough times. Whether you're facing a personal challenge or dealing with stress, having someone who listens, empathizes, and offers encouragement can make all the difference in how you approach and overcome difficulties.
- **Inspiration and Growth**: When you surround yourself with people who are also striving for growth, positivity, and success, you are more likely to push yourself in the same direction. Positive relationships serve as sources of inspiration, challenging you to aim higher and think more expansively.
- **Accountability Partners**: It's easy to slip back into old patterns of negative thinking, especially when life gets tough. Having people who hold you accountable for maintaining a positive mindset is invaluable. Whether it's a friend, mentor, or coach, an accountability partner can remind you of your goals and encourage you to keep going, even when the going gets tough.

Building a Positive Community

Creating and sustaining positive relationships requires conscious effort. Here are a few strategies for building a supportive, growth-oriented community:

1. **Seek Like-Minded Individuals**: Surround yourself with people who share your values and goals. Whether through professional networks, personal friendships, or online communities, it's essential to connect with individuals who understand your journey and support your personal growth.
2. **Engage in Meaningful Conversations**: Relationships are strengthened through meaningful, authentic conversations. Take time to nurture your connections by discussing topics

that inspire, uplift, and challenge both of you to think positively.
3. **Offer and Seek Support**: Relationships are reciprocal. Be willing to offer support when others need it, and don't be afraid to ask for help when you're struggling. Mutual support builds trust and deepens connections, creating a strong foundation for positivity.

How to Set Boundaries with Negativity (People, Media, Habits)

One of the most critical aspects of maintaining a positive mindset is setting firm boundaries with sources of negativity. This includes not only people but also the media you consume and the habits you engage in. Setting boundaries isn't about isolating yourself or avoiding reality; it's about protecting your mental and emotional well-being so that you can thrive.

Managing Negative Relationships

- **Identify Energy Drainers**: Some people consistently drain your energy, whether through constant complaints, criticism, or drama. While you can't always cut these people out of your life (especially if they are family or co-workers), you can set boundaries. Limit your interactions with them, and protect your emotional space by not engaging in their negativity.
- **Assertive Communication**: It's essential to communicate your boundaries clearly and assertively. For example, if a friend or colleague continually brings up negative topics, politely but firmly steer the conversation in a more positive direction. You might say, "I understand you're frustrated, but can we focus on solutions instead of the problems?"
- **Distance and Detachment**: In some cases, it's necessary to distance yourself from toxic individuals who are unwilling or unable to change. This doesn't mean cutting them off completely, but rather, creating emotional distance so that their negativity doesn't affect you as deeply.

Media Consumption: A Hidden Source of Negativity

- **Curate Your Media Diet**: We live in an age of information overload, and much of the media we consume is filled with fear, sensationalism, and negativity. Be selective about the news, social media, and entertainment you engage with. Choose sources that inspire and inform you rather than

overwhelm or stress you.
- **Social Media Boundaries**: Social media can be a double-edged sword. While it can connect you to positive communities, it can also expose you to negativity, comparison, and unrealistic expectations. Set time limits on your social media use, unfollow accounts that make you feel inadequate, and follow pages that promote positivity and growth.

Breaking Negative Habits
- **Identify Self-Sabotaging Behaviours**: We all have habits that don't serve us—whether it's procrastination, negative self-talk, or unhealthy lifestyle choices. These habits often feed into a negative mindset. Start by identifying these behaviours and their triggers, and then gradually work on replacing them with healthier alternatives.
- **Create Positive Rituals**: Replace negative habits with positive ones that nurture your well-being. For example, if you notice that you start your day by scrolling through negative news, replace that with a morning gratitude practice or a quick meditation session. Small positive rituals can have a compounding effect on your overall mindset.

Building a Supportive Network That Fosters Growth

Creating a supportive network that fosters growth and positivity requires intention and effort. Here's how to build a circle of individuals who will uplift, challenge, and inspire you on your journey towards a more positive life.

Seek Out Growth-Oriented Communities
- **Join Groups or Organizations**: Whether it's a professional organization, a local club, or an online community, seek out groups where people are focused on personal development, growth, and positivity. These spaces provide opportunities to connect with like-minded individuals who can offer support and share their experiences.
- **Mentorship and Coaching**: Having a mentor or coach who believes in your potential and pushes you to be your best can be transformative. A good mentor provides guidance, feedback, and encouragement, helping you navigate challenges and stay committed to your goals.
- **Participate Actively**: Building a supportive network is a

two-way street. Participate actively in the communities you join. Offer support, share your knowledge, and celebrate others' successes. The more you invest in your relationships, the more you'll get out of them.

Practice Gratitude in Relationships

- **Appreciate and Acknowledge**: Gratitude is a powerful tool for strengthening relationships. Take time to appreciate the people in your life who support and uplift you. A simple thank-you note, a word of encouragement, or an acknowledgment of someone's impact on your life can go a long way in fostering positive, supportive connections.

In conclusion, surrounding yourself with positivity is not a passive process; it's a conscious, ongoing effort to design your environment, relationships, and habits in a way that nurtures your growth. By curating your physical and social environment, setting boundaries with negativity, and building a community that supports your goals, you create the ideal conditions for a positive mindset to flourish. And remember, just as a garden needs regular care, so too does your mental and emotional environment. With consistent attention and nurturing, you can cultivate a life filled with positivity, growth, and joy.

10 Powerful Examples

Here are 10 powerful examples of how to be positive around people while exuding confidence and energy.

1. Active Listening with Empathy

Being genuinely present in conversations is a powerful way to build connections and show confidence. When people feel heard, they are more likely to engage with you positively.

How to Do It: Instead of thinking about what to say next, focus entirely on the person speaking. Nod to show understanding, ask follow-up questions, and summarize what they've said. Empathy is key, so try to see the situation from their perspective without rushing to offer solutions.

The Power Behind It: Active listening shows emotional intelligence and builds trust, making you more relatable and empowering others to open up. Confidence isn't about always leading the conversation; it's about being comfortable enough to let others take the stage.

Shifting Mindsets

2. Use Positive Body Language

Your body language often speaks louder than words. Maintaining open and welcoming body language conveys confidence and positivity.

How to Do It: Stand tall with your shoulders back and keep your posture relaxed. Make eye contact, smile genuinely, and avoid crossing your arms, which can appear closed off. Use gestures to emphasize points but ensure they're natural and not forced.

The Power Behind It: Positive body language can make people feel at ease around you and conveys that you are approachable and in control. Confident body language projects authority without saying a word.

3. Compliment with Sincerity

A well-placed compliment can uplift others and show that you notice and appreciate their efforts or qualities.

How to Do It: Instead of generic compliments like "You're great," get specific. Mention something unique about them, like "I admire how calm you stay under pressure" or "Your presentation was really engaging and clear."

The Power behind It: When compliments are genuine, they not only make the other person feel good, but they also position you as someone who is thoughtful and observant. Offering positive reinforcement boosts your leadership and influence.

4. Speak with Positive Energy

Your tone and choice of words have a significant impact on how others perceive you. Speaking with energy and optimism can change the entire atmosphere of a conversation.

How to Do It: Replace negative language with positive phrasing. Instead of "I'm not sure this will work," say, "I believe we can find a way to make this work." Use uplifting language like "excited," "grateful," and "motivated" to express your outlook.

The Power Behind It: Positivity in speech shows that you are proactive and solution-oriented, which boosts your credibility and makes you a source of encouragement for others. This builds your reputation as someone who brings good energy into any room.

5. Embrace Vulnerability with Confidence

Being vulnerable can seem counterintuitive to confidence, but true power comes from authenticity. Sharing personal experiences, including challenges, can build deeper connections.

How to Do It: When appropriate, share a time when you

overcame a difficulty or made a mistake. Frame it as a learning experience, focusing on the growth rather than the struggle. For example, "I used to struggle with public speaking, but I worked on it by practicing daily."

The Power behind It: Vulnerability shows strength because it demonstrates self-awareness and courage. It humanizes you, making you more relatable and trustworthy, and people respect those who can admit imperfection while showcasing resilience.

6. Radiate Gratitude

Gratitude is one of the simplest yet most impactful ways to maintain a positive mindset and uplift others.

How to Do It: Make it a habit to express gratitude regularly, whether it's thanking someone for their help, acknowledging their hard work, or simply appreciating their presence in your life. Try saying things like, "I really appreciate how much effort you put into this project."

The Power behind It: Gratitude shifts your focus from what's lacking to what's abundant, and expressing it strengthens your relationships. People naturally gravitate toward those who appreciate them, enhancing your influence and the positive energy you exude.

7. Maintain Composure in Stressful Situations

Remaining calm under pressure is a sign of strength and positivity. When others see you handling stress with grace, they'll be inspired to do the same.

How to Do It: Practice mindfulness and breathing exercises to manage stress. In challenging moments, pause before reacting and consider the best way forward. Respond calmly and with intention, rather than reacting impulsively.

The Power behind It: Keeping your cool not only shows emotional maturity but also projects confidence and reliability. People will look to you as a source of stability and level-headedness, which strengthens your leadership qualities.

8. Encourage and Empower Others

One of the most powerful ways to be positive around people is to empower them. When you lift others up, you create a ripple effect of positivity.

How to Do It: Offer words of encouragement when someone is facing a challenge or unsure of their abilities. Say things like, "I believe you have the skills to accomplish this," or "You're capable of great things."

Shifting Mindsets

The Power Behind It: Encouraging others shows that you're secure in yourself and willing to share your success. This creates a supportive environment where people feel motivated and confident in your presence, boosting your influence and strengthening relationships.

9. Be Consistent in Your Actions and Words

Consistency builds trust and reinforces the positive image you want to project. People need to know they can rely on you to stay true to your word.

How to Do It: Follow through on promises and commitments, no matter how small. Be someone who keeps their word. If you say you'll attend an event or deliver something on a deadline, do it. Avoid being inconsistent with your mood or behaviour.

The Power behind It: Consistency builds a reputation of reliability and trustworthiness. When people know they can count on you, they'll respect and admire you more, creating stronger bonds of trust and loyalty.

10. Celebrate Others' Successes

Acknowledging and celebrating the success of others doesn't diminish your own. It shows confidence in your abilities and a genuinely positive mindset.

How to Do It: When someone achieves something significant, take the time to celebrate their success. Say, "I'm so happy for your accomplishment! You've worked really hard, and it shows." Participate in their joy, and avoid any feelings of competition or envy.

The Power behind It: Celebrating others' achievements reinforces your positivity and creates a culture of mutual respect and encouragement. It also shows that you are secure enough in your own success to genuinely uplift others, which is a sign of true confidence and leadership.

Being positive around others while showing confidence and power is about creating an authentic, uplifting energy that draws people to you. By mastering these techniques—active listening, positive body language, vulnerability, gratitude, and more—you'll inspire, motivate, and build deeper, more meaningful connections with the people around you.

CHAPTER 7. OVERCOMING OBSTACLES TO POSITIVE THINKING

As a professional life coach, one of the greatest challenges people face in their personal development is shifting to a positive mindset, especially when life's circumstances seem to conspire against them. Whether it's self-doubt, fear, or the lingering memory of past failures, maintaining a positive mindset can sometimes feel like an uphill battle. However, learning how to overcome these obstacles is not only possible but can be life-changing. The key is understanding that positive thinking is not about ignoring challenges but approaching them with the right tools, mindset, and strategies.

In this chapter, we'll dive deep into the common challenges that arise when adopting a positive mindset, how to tackle negativity constructively, and how to develop resilience to maintain positivity through tough times. By the end of this chapter, you'll not only be equipped to overcome the obstacles to positive thinking but also feel empowered to inspire others to do the same.

Common Challenges to Shifting to a Positive Mindset

One of the biggest misconceptions about positive thinking is that it's simply about "thinking happy thoughts" or denying the existence of challenges. However, true positivity involves facing those challenges head-on while maintaining the belief that you have the strength and resources to overcome them. Several common challenges can arise when trying to shift into this mindset, and understanding them is the first step toward mastering them.

1. Self-Doubt

Self-doubt is the inner critic that questions your abilities, worth, and potential. It's one of the most common obstacles to positive thinking, and it can manifest as imposter syndrome, feelings of inadequacy, or a constant comparison to others.

Understanding Self-Doubt: Self-doubt often stems from early life experiences where failure or mistakes were met with criticism rather than encouragement. Over time, this internalized criticism becomes the voice of doubt that undermines your confidence.

How to Overcome Self-Doubt:
- **Practice Self-Compassion**: Instead of berating yourself for every mistake, practice treating yourself with kindness

and understanding. Remember, every successful person has faced setbacks and self-doubt. The difference is that they pushed through it.

- **Challenge Negative Self-Talk**: Whenever a doubtful thought creeps in, counter it with a positive affirmation or remind yourself of past successes. For example, if the thought is "I'm not good enough to achieve this," challenge it with "I've overcome difficult challenges before, and I can do it again."
- **Take Action**: Action is the antidote to doubt. Often, taking the first step, even if it's small, can silence the inner critic. Break your goals into manageable pieces and celebrate each accomplishment.

2. Fear of Failure

Fear of failure can be paralyzing. It stops people from taking risks, pursuing dreams, or even making small changes in their lives. The fear is often rooted in the belief that failure is a reflection of who you are rather than an opportunity to learn.

Understanding the Fear of Failure: At its core, the fear of failure is often tied to the fear of judgment from others or the feeling of personal inadequacy. We fear that if we fail, we will be seen as "less than," unworthy, or incapable.

How to Overcome Fear of Failure:

- **Redefine Failure**: Instead of seeing failure as the end, view it as a stepping stone toward success. Every failure is a learning experience that brings you closer to your goal. The most successful people often talk about how many times they've failed before they found the right path.
- **Visualize Success**: Visualization is a powerful tool. Instead of focusing on what could go wrong, spend time imagining what will happen when things go right. Visualize yourself succeeding and basking in the rewards of your hard work.
- **Take Calculated Risks**: Risk is inherent in growth. Instead of avoiding risk altogether, learn how to take calculated risks where the potential benefits outweigh the downsides. Remember, even a small step forward is better than standing still.

3. Past Failures

Many people are haunted by past failures, and these experiences can create mental barriers that prevent them from embracing a positive mindset. The memory of a failed business, relationship, or personal endeavour can make it difficult to believe in future success.

Understanding the Impact of Past Failures: Past failures leave emotional scars. These experiences are often relived mentally, reinforcing a narrative of defeat and reinforcing the belief that failure will happen again.

How to Overcome the Weight of Past Failures:
- **Rewrite Your Narrative**: Instead of allowing your past failures to define you, reframe them as part of your growth journey. What lessons did you learn? How did those failures make you stronger or wiser? You are not your past mistakes; you are what you've learned from them.
- **Forgive Yourself**: Self-forgiveness is essential. Let go of the guilt and shame associated with past failures. Recognize that you were doing your best with the knowledge and resources you had at the time.
- **Set New Goals**: Break free from the past by setting new, exciting goals for your future. When you are focused on where you are going rather than where you've been, you'll have less mental energy for dwelling on past mistakes.

How to Tackle Pessimism, Criticism, and Negative Feedback Constructively

Negative thinking can be pervasive, whether it's from your inner critic, external criticism from others, or feedback that feels harsh. However, learning how to tackle these challenges head-on can transform them into opportunities for growth and deeper positivity.

1. Dealing with Your Own Pessimism

It's natural to have negative thoughts from time to time, but chronic pessimism can become a major roadblock to positive thinking. Pessimistic thoughts are often automatic and habitual, but they can be challenged and changed.

Steps to Overcome Pessimism:
- **Catch Negative Thoughts Early**: Pay attention to your thoughts. Whenever a pessimistic thought arises, ask yourself if it's based on facts or assumptions. Often, pessimistic thoughts are distortions of reality.
- **Practice Gratitude**: Gratitude is a proven antidote to negativity. Take time each day to reflect on what's going well in your life. Focus on the positives, no matter how small,

and you'll slowly rewire your brain to look for the good.
- **Surround Yourself with Positivity**: Limit your exposure to negative media, environments, and conversations. If certain people in your life tend to bring you down, set boundaries. Actively seek out positive influences, whether it's through reading inspiring books, listening to motivational podcasts, or spending time with uplifting people.

2. Responding to External Criticism

Criticism can feel like a personal attack, but not all criticism is bad. When handled correctly, constructive feedback can help you grow. The key is to differentiate between constructive criticism and harmful criticism and respond appropriately.

How to Handle Criticism:
- **Listen Without Reacting**: When receiving criticism, avoid reacting defensively. Take a deep breath, listen to what's being said, and try to understand the other person's perspective.
- **Extract the Useful**: Not all criticism is valid, but even in the harshest feedback, there's often a nugget of truth. Ask yourself, "What can I learn from this?" and use that lesson to improve.
- **Set Boundaries with Harmful Criticism**: If someone is being overly harsh or attacking you rather than offering helpful feedback, it's important to set boundaries. You can say something like, "I appreciate your input, but I don't think this conversation is productive right now."

Dealing with Setbacks and Failures in a Positive Way

Setbacks are an inevitable part of life, and how you respond to them can either propel you forward or keep you stuck. Developing resilience and learning how to maintain positivity in the face of failure is key to long-term success.

1. Reframe Setbacks as Learning Opportunities

When something doesn't go as planned, it's easy to fall into the trap of disappointment or self-blame. However, setbacks are often the best teachers.

How to Reframe Setbacks:
- **Ask Constructive Questions**: Instead of asking, "Why did this happen to me?" ask, "What can I learn from this?" or

"How can I improve next time?"
- **Focus on What You Can Control**: Setbacks often involve factors beyond your control. Instead of fixating on what went wrong, focus on what's within your power to change or improve.
- **Celebrate Effort, Not Just Results**: Even if the outcome wasn't what you hoped for, celebrate the effort you put in. Acknowledge your hard work and use it as fuel to try again.

2. Develop a Resilient Mindset

Resilience is the ability to bounce back from adversity, and it's a skill that can be developed with practice. Resilient people view setbacks as temporary and solvable, and they maintain a long-term perspective.

How to Build Resilience:
- **Embrace Challenges**: Don't shy away from difficult situations. The more you face adversity, the stronger you become. Each challenge is an opportunity to build mental and emotional strength.
- **Maintain a Growth Mindset**: A growth mindset is the belief that your abilities can be developed through effort and learning. Instead of seeing failure as a reflection of your capabilities, see it as a chance to grow.
- **Develop Healthy Coping Mechanisms**: When faced with tough times, it's important to have healthy coping strategies in place. This could include exercise, journaling, meditation, or talking to a supportive friend.

Strategies to Maintain Positivity during Tough Times

Maintaining a positive mindset during difficult periods is one of the greatest challenges to personal growth, but it's also when positivity is most needed. Here are some strategies to stay positive when life gets tough.

1. Practice Mindfulness and Meditation

Mindfulness helps you stay grounded in the present moment rather than getting caught up in worries about the future or regrets about the past.

How to Practice Mindfulness:
- **Start with Breathing Exercises**: Deep, mindful breathing can instantly calm your mind and help you refocus. Try taking five deep breaths, inhaling for four counts, holding

Shifting Mindsets

for four counts, and exhaling for four counts.
- **Focus on the Present Moment**: Whether you're eating, walking, or working, pay attention to the sensations around you. Notice the texture of your food, the sound of your footsteps, or the feel of your keyboard. This practice trains your brain to stay present, reducing stress and anxiety.

2. Cultivate a Support System

During tough times, it's essential to lean on a strong support network. Whether it's friends, family, or a mentor, having people to turn to can make all the difference.

How to Build a Support System:
- **Identify Positive Influences**: Surround yourself with people who uplift and inspire you. Avoid toxic relationships that drain your energy or reinforce negative thinking.
- **Don't Be Afraid to Ask for Help**: When you're struggling, reach out to those who care about you. Asking for help is not a sign of weakness; it's a sign of strength and self-awareness.

3. Keep a Gratitude Journal

Gratitude shifts your focus from what's lacking to what's abundant, and it's a powerful tool for maintaining positivity.

How to Keep a Gratitude Journal:
- **Write Daily**: Every day, write down three things you're grateful for, no matter how small. It could be something as simple as enjoying a cup of coffee or receiving a kind message from a friend.
- **Reflect on Difficult Situations**: Even in challenging times, there's always something to be grateful for. Reflect on what you're learning from the experience and how it's helping you grow.

Overcoming the obstacles to positive thinking isn't about denying difficulties or pretending that everything is perfect. It's about shifting your perspective and equipping yourself with the tools to face challenges head-on while maintaining a hopeful and constructive mindset. By learning to overcome self-doubt, fear, past failures, and negativity, you'll be able to foster a mindset of growth, resilience, and positivity that can carry you through even the toughest of times.

CHAPTER 8. THE POWER OF GRATITUDE AND MINDFULNESS

In a world that often feels chaotic and overwhelming, the simple practices of gratitude and mindfulness can be transformative. These practices aren't just about feeling good in the moment; they are scientifically proven methods that rewire your brain, improve your emotional resilience, and help you maintain a positive outlook. As a life coach, I've seen first-hand how adopting a gratitude and mindfulness routine can create a profound shift in both mindset and behaviour, leading to greater happiness, success, and fulfilment.

In this chapter, we'll dive into the science behind gratitude and mindfulness, explore practical exercises for incorporating these habits into your daily life, and show you how to build a routine that keeps you grounded and focused on the present. If you're looking to elevate your positivity and well-being, these practices are essential tools on your journey.

The Science of Gratitude and How It Enhances Positivity

Gratitude is more than just saying "thank you" when something good happens. It is a powerful emotional state that alters the brain's chemistry and wiring, enhancing positivity, reducing stress, and increasing overall life satisfaction. Understanding the science behind gratitude helps to appreciate its true power and why it has such a profound impact on our lives.

1. Gratitude Rewires the Brain for Positivity

Research has shown that gratitude practices have a measurable impact on brain function. When we focus on things we are grateful for, the brain releases dopamine and serotonin—two neurotransmitters responsible for feelings of happiness and pleasure. These "feel-good" chemicals activate areas of the brain associated with emotional regulation and contentment, which leads to a more positive overall mindset.

Key Studies on Gratitude:
- A landmark study by Rd. Robert A. Emmons, a leading gratitude researcher, found that individuals who kept a daily gratitude journal experienced higher levels of optimism, felt better about their lives, and exercised more.
- Neuroscientist Alex Korb has demonstrated how gratitude

increases neural sensitivity in the prefrontal cortex, a brain region responsible for managing emotions and decision-making. This improved brain function helps individuals cope better with stress and anxiety.

2. Gratitude Reduces Stress and Improves Mental Health

One of the most profound effects of practicing gratitude is its ability to reduce stress and improve mental health. In today's fast-paced world, chronic stress is a widespread problem that contributes to anxiety, depression, and burnout. However, gratitude helps to counteract these effects by shifting our focus away from what's going wrong to what is going right in our lives.

How Gratitude Reduces Stress:

- **Physiological Effects**: Gratitude lowers levels of cortisol, the stress hormone. Chronic stress elevates cortisol, leading to physical and emotional exhaustion. Gratitude helps regulate cortisol, reducing its harmful effects and promoting relaxation.
- **Emotional Resilience**: Practicing gratitude increases emotional resilience, which is the ability to bounce back from adversity. By focusing on what you have rather than what you lack, you cultivate an inner strength that helps you cope with challenges more effectively.

3. Gratitude Enhances Relationships and Social Bonds

Gratitude isn't just an internal practice; it also impacts our relationships with others. Expressing gratitude to those around us strengthens social bonds, enhances trust, and fosters a deeper sense of connection.

The Social Science of Gratitude:

- Gratitude encourages pro-social behaviour. People who practice gratitude are more likely to help others, show empathy, and maintain supportive relationships. This creates a positive feedback loop—when we express gratitude, others feel appreciated, which strengthens the bond and makes them more likely to reciprocate.
- Research conducted by the Greater Good Science Centre at UC Berkeley found that couples who express gratitude toward each other feel more positive about their relationship and more connected to one another.

Practical Exercises for Practicing Gratitude Daily

While the benefits of gratitude are clear, it's important to incorporate specific, practical exercises into your daily life to truly experience its impact. Let's explore several effective ways to practice gratitude that can easily fit into any routine.

1. The Gratitude Journal

One of the most effective and popular methods for cultivating gratitude is keeping a daily gratitude journal. This exercise helps you focus on the positive aspects of your day and trains your brain to notice the good more frequently.

How to Keep a Gratitude Journal:

- **Consistency**: Set aside 5 to 10 minutes each day, preferably in the morning or before bed, to reflect on what you are grateful for. Write down at least three things—big or small—that you appreciated during the day.
- **Specificity**: Be as specific as possible. Instead of writing, "I'm grateful for my family," try, "I'm grateful for the kind words my partner said to me when I was feeling stressed." Specific examples help you relive positive moments and strengthen the emotional impact.
- **Reflect on Challenges**: Include moments of difficulty and how they contributed to your growth. For example, "I'm grateful for the challenging project at work because it taught me new skills."

2. Gratitude Letters

Writing gratitude letters to people who have positively impacted your life is a powerful way to deepen your sense of thankfulness and strengthen your relationships. It is also an incredibly moving experience for the recipient.

How to Write a Gratitude Letter:

- **Choose Someone Meaningful**: Think of a person who has had a significant positive impact on your life—someone who has supported you, taught you, or made a difference.
- **Be Detailed and Sincere**: Write about specific moments where their actions touched your life. Share how their kindness, advice, or support made you feel and what it meant to you.
- **Deliver the Letter**: If possible, deliver the letter in person. Witnessing the recipient's reaction enhances the emotional experience for both of you, reinforcing feelings of

connection and gratitude.

3. Gratitude Walks

Combining physical movement with a gratitude practice amplifies the benefits. Taking a "gratitude walk" is an excellent way to connect with nature, clear your mind, and practice gratitude simultaneously.

How to Practice a Gratitude Walk:
- **Choose a Peaceful Environment**: Find a park, trail, or Quiet Street where you can walk without distractions.
- **Focus on the Present Moment**: As you walk, bring your attention to the sensations around you—the sound of birds, the rustling of leaves, the feel of the sun or wind on your skin. Be present.
- **Reflect on What You're Grateful For**: With each step, mentally list things you are grateful for. These could be related to your environment, your personal life, or even small moments of joy you experienced recently.

How Mindfulness Helps in Staying Present and Reducing Negative Thinking

Mindfulness is the practice of staying fully present in the moment, without judgment. By focusing on the here and now, you reduce the tendency to dwell on past regrets or future anxieties. Mindfulness plays a crucial role in reducing negative thinking and cultivating a positive mindset.

1. The Power of the Present Moment

Mindfulness teaches us that the present moment is all we truly have. Worrying about the future or ruminating over the past only takes us away from the richness of the now.

Why the Present Moment Matters:
- **Reduced Anxiety**: Anxiety often stems from worrying about the future—whether it's fear of failure, uncertainty, or concerns about things beyond our control. By focusing on the present, mindfulness helps quiet these worries and bring peace to the mind.
- **Increased Awareness**: Mindfulness heightens your awareness of your thoughts, emotions, and surroundings. When you are fully present, you can observe your thoughts without being controlled by them. This allows you to catch negative thought patterns and redirect them before they spiral.

2. Mindfulness as a Tool for Managing Negative Emotions

Negative thinking often arises from automatic, unexamined thought patterns. These can be triggered by stress, past traumas, or difficult situations. Mindfulness helps you interrupt these patterns and replace them with constructive, positive thinking.

How Mindfulness Interrupts Negative Thoughts:

- **Non-Reactivity**: When practicing mindfulness, you learn to observe your thoughts and feelings without immediately reacting to them. Instead of letting a negative thought snowball, you can acknowledge it, let it pass, and refocus on the present.
- **Emotional Regulation**: Mindfulness improves emotional regulation by increasing activity in the prefrontal cortex (the part of the brain responsible for decision-making and self-control) and reducing activity in the amygdala (the brain's fear centre). This makes it easier to stay calm and composed in the face of stress.

Building a Gratitude and Mindfulness Routine

To truly reap the benefits of gratitude and mindfulness, it's important to make these practices part of your daily life. By creating a structured routine, you ensure that these habits become automatic, leading to lasting positive change.

1. Start Small, Build Gradually

It's easy to feel overwhelmed when trying to build new habits, especially when life is busy. The key to success is starting small and gradually increasing your commitment as the practices become part of your daily rhythm.

How to Build Your Routine:

- **Set a Specific Time**: Choose a specific time each day to practice gratitude and mindfulness. For example, you could journal for five minutes each morning or meditate for 10 minutes before bed.
- **Use Reminders**: Set reminders on your phone or create a visual cue, such as a post it notes on your mirror, to prompt you to engage in your gratitude or mindfulness practice.
- **Track Your Progress**: Keep a simple habit tracker to note when you've completed your gratitude journaling or mindfulness meditation for the day. Tracking your progress helps build consistency and motivates you to stay on track.

2. Combine Gratitude and Mindfulness Practices

You don't have to practice gratitude and mindfulness separately. In fact, combining them can amplify their benefits.

Integrating Gratitude and Mindfulness:
- **Mindful Gratitude Meditation**: During your mindfulness meditation, focus on things you're grateful for. As you sit quietly, let your mind reflect on specific moments or people who have brought joy or meaning to your life.
- **Gratitude Mindfulness in Daily Activities**: Throughout your day, practice mindful gratitude. Whether you're washing dishes, walking, or commuting, bring your attention to the present moment and reflect on what you're grateful for in that moment.

Gratitude and mindfulness are life-changing practices that can transform how you experience the world. By understanding the science behind these tools and committing to practical exercises, you can build a routine that fosters lasting positivity, emotional resilience, and inner peace. As a life coach, I've seen these practices help individuals shift their mindset from scarcity to abundance, from anxiety to calm, and from stress to joy. Make the choice today to embrace gratitude and mindfulness, and watch as your life begins to shift in powerful, positive ways.

10 Tips for Financial Freedom: Saving Money, Investing in Yourself, and Building a Future

Achieving financial freedom is not just about having money—it's about using your resources wisely to create the life you want, both personally and professionally. Whether you're aiming to save more, invest in your future, or grow your business, financial freedom is possible with the right mindset and strategies. Here are 10 actionable tips to help you reach that goal.

1. Create a Solid Financial Plan with Clear Goals

Financial freedom starts with clarity. You need a roadmap to get where you want to go. A detailed financial plan provides direction and allows you to measure progress over time.
- **Set specific goals**: Determine your short-term, medium-term, and long-term financial objectives. For example, you might aim to save $10,000 within the next year, buy a house in five years, or retire at 55.
- **Track your spending**: Review your income and expenses

to understand where your money is going. Use apps or budgeting software to help track spending habits and spot areas where you can cut back.
- **Allocate your funds**: Divide your income into categories like savings, investments, emergency funds, and personal spending. Having a clear plan ensures you consistently work towards your financial goals.

2. Prioritize Saving a Percentage of Your Income

One of the most important habits for financial independence is consistently saving a portion of your income. Start with whatever percentage you can afford and gradually increase it as your financial situation improves.
- **Automate your savings**: Set up automatic transfers to a savings account. This "pay yourself first" strategy ensures that you prioritize your financial future before spending on discretionary items.
- **Build an emergency fund**: Save 3-6 months' worth of living expenses in an emergency fund to protect yourself from unexpected financial challenges, such as job loss or medical emergencies.
- **Set specific savings goals**: Have clear targets, whether it's saving for a vacation, an investment, or a new business venture. Breaking down savings goals into manageable amounts makes them easier to achieve.

3. Invest in Personal Development and Skill-Building

Your most valuable asset is yourself. By continuously improving your skills, you increase your earning potential and open up new opportunities. Financial freedom often comes from having multiple income streams and valuable skills that set you apart in the market.
- **Take online courses**: Invest in courses that enhance your professional skills, whether it's in leadership, digital marketing, project management, or a specialized trade.
- **Attend seminars and workshops**: Live events provide access to industry experts, cutting-edge ideas, and opportunities for networking.
- **Focus on skills with a high ROI**: Learning high-demand skills, such as coding, financial management, or digital marketing, can greatly enhance your career or business profitability.

Shifting Mindsets

4. Diversify Your Income Streams

Relying on a single source of income can be risky. Diversifying your income streams allows you to spread risk, build wealth faster, and move closer to financial freedom.

- **Start a side business**: Consider starting a side hustle that aligns with your interests and expertise. Whether it's freelancing, consulting, or selling products online, a second income stream boosts financial security.
- **Invest in income-generating assets**: Real estate, stocks, or dividend-paying investments can provide additional income. Choose investments that match your risk tolerance and financial goals.
- **Monetize a hobby**: Turn a passion or hobby into a small business, such as photography, writing, or fitness coaching. This can supplement your income while allowing you to do something you love.

5. Live Below Your Means and Avoid Lifestyle Inflation

Many people increase their spending as their income rises, a phenomenon known as lifestyle inflation. Avoiding this trap is key to long-term financial freedom.

- **Stick to a budget**: Even as you earn more, maintain a budget that prioritizes saving and investing. Don't feel the need to upgrade your lifestyle just because you can afford to.
- **Be mindful of expenses**: Regularly audit your expenses to see where you can cut costs without sacrificing quality of life. This could include cancelling unused subscriptions, negotiating better deals on bills, or shopping more consciously.
- **Avoid unnecessary debt**: Debt can derail your financial progress, especially if it's for non-essential items. Prioritize paying off high-interest debt like credit cards, and avoid financing items that don't contribute to your long-term wealth.

6. Invest for the Long-Term and Start Early

Investing is one of the most effective ways to grow your wealth and achieve financial freedom. The earlier you start, the more time your investments have to grow, thanks to the power of compound interest.

- **Maximize retirement contributions**: Contribute to

retirement accounts such as a 401(k), IRA, or other tax-advantaged accounts. These accounts allow your money to grow tax-free or tax-deferred.

- **Diversify your investment portfolio**: Spread your investments across various asset classes (stocks, bonds, real estate, etc.) to reduce risk. A diversified portfolio helps protect against market volatility.
- **Invest consistently**: Whether the market is up or down, keep investing. Dollar-cost averaging, where you invest a fixed amount regularly, helps you take advantage of market fluctuations and reduces the risk of investing all your money at a market high.

7. Invest in Your Business or Start One

Building or investing in your own business can be a path to both financial freedom and personal fulfilment. With the right strategy, a business can generate long-term wealth and provide a lifestyle you control.

- **Start small and scale**: If you have an entrepreneurial spirit, start with a small business that requires minimal startup capital. As it becomes profitable, reinvest the earnings to scale and grow.
- **Develop multiple revenue streams**: Whether you're a freelancer or run a full-scale business, diversifying your services or product lines can create additional revenue streams and safeguard against market shifts.
- **Reinvest profits wisely**: Use business profits to reinvest in growth, whether that's through marketing, hiring skilled employees, or expanding your product offerings. This not only helps the business grow but also builds long-term wealth for you.

8. Leverage Technology for Financial Growth

Harnessing the power of technology can accelerate your journey to financial freedom. From smart apps to investment platforms, the digital world offers countless tools to help you save, invest, and grow.

- **Use budgeting apps**: Apps like Mint, YNAB (You Need a Budget), or Pocket Guard can help you stay on top of your spending, saving, and financial goals.
- **Automate investments**: Robo-advisors like Betterment or Wealth front can help you automate your investments,

balancing your portfolio based on your risk tolerance and financial objectives.
- **Explore passive income options**: Use platforms like Etsy, Shopify, or Amazon to create an online business, or invest in digital real estate like websites or blogs that generate passive income.

9. Stay Educated on Personal Finance and Business Trends

To build financial freedom, you need to stay informed about changes in personal finance and business landscapes. Continual learning will give you the knowledge and confidence to make smart financial decisions.

- **Read financial books and blogs**: Follow personal finance experts like Dave Ramsey or Suze Orman, and regularly read financial news from trusted sources such as Forbes or CNBC.
- **Join financial or entrepreneurial communities**: Engage with groups or forums where you can discuss financial strategies, investment ideas, or business opportunities. Networking with like-minded individuals can provide valuable insights and opportunities.
- **Learn from your mistakes**: Every financial misstep is an opportunity to learn. Reflect on past decisions, understand what went wrong, and use those lessons to make better choices in the future.

10. Plan for the Future: Retirement and Legacy Building

Financial freedom also means planning for a future where you no longer need to work for money. Building wealth for retirement and leaving a legacy ensures that your financial freedom extends beyond your working years.

- **Create a retirement plan**: Whether you want to retire early or enjoy a comfortable retirement later, have a plan in place. Maximize your contributions to retirement accounts and consider other investment vehicles like real estate or annuities.
- **Invest in passive income for retirement**: Look for investments that will provide steady income in retirement, such as rental properties, dividend-paying stocks, or business ventures that can run without your constant involvement.
- **Think about your legacy**: Financial freedom isn't just

Shifting Mindsets

about you. Consider how you want to leave a legacy for future generations, whether through investments, charitable contributions, or passing down a family business.

Financial freedom is a journey that requires discipline, education, and smart decision-making. By adopting these tips—whether it's prioritizing savings, investing in yourself and your business, or planning for your future—you'll be well on your way to creating a life of financial security, freedom, and endless possibilities. With each step, you're not just building wealth; you're building a future that aligns with your values, goals, and dreams.

CHAPTER 9. SUSTAINING LONG-TERM POSITIVITY

Positivity is more than just a fleeting emotion or momentary boost in mood—it's a lifestyle choice, a mindset you can cultivate and maintain long-term. Achieving sustained positivity requires dedication, mindfulness, and self-awareness. In this chapter, we'll explore how to make positivity a lasting part of your life, rather than a temporary phase, by developing a plan, focusing on self-improvement, and staying motivated.

How to Make Positivity a Lifestyle Rather Than a Temporary Phase

Positivity, like any meaningful pursuit, requires consistent effort to become a core part of your life. Many people experience moments of positive thinking but struggle to sustain this mindset long-term, especially when life presents challenges. So how do you move from experiencing short bursts of positivity to living a life deeply rooted in it?

1. Understand the Nature of Positivity as a Habit

First and foremost, positivity is a habit—one that you can cultivate with conscious effort. Like any habit, it takes time to form but can become automatic with repetition.

- **Start with small daily changes**: Incorporating small, positive habits into your day can create a ripple effect. For instance, expressing gratitude every morning, complimenting someone, or reframing a negative thought into a positive one are tiny shifts that add up over time.
- **Focus on the internal, not the external**: True positivity comes from within and isn't dependent on external circumstances. It's about your reaction to situations rather than the situations themselves. This internal focus strengthens your ability to remain positive, even when life isn't perfect.

2. Align Your Positivity with Your Values and Beliefs

Living a life of positivity isn't about faking happiness. It's about aligning your mindset with your core values, beliefs, and the vision you have for your life.

- **Identify your core values**: Take time to reflect on the principles that matter most to you—integrity, kindness, growth, service, or compassion, for example. When your actions align with these values, positivity becomes natural because you're living authentically.

- **Make decisions based on your values**: Consistently making choices that reflect your values reinforces a positive life. If you value growth, embrace challenges as opportunities for learning. If you value relationships, focus on spreading kindness and empathy.

3. Shift Your Mindset from Reactive to Proactive

Rather than allowing external circumstances to dictate your mood, learn to respond proactively to life's events.

- **Control your inner dialogue**: Your thoughts shape your reality. By becoming aware of negative self-talk and deliberately changing it, you can influence how you feel. Instead of "I can't handle this," try "I'll find a way through this."
- **Practice emotional resilience**: Positivity doesn't mean ignoring negative emotions. Instead, practice resilience by accepting these feelings and then shifting your focus to what you can learn or how you can grow from the situation.

Creating a Personal Action Plan for Maintaining a Positive Mindset

Sustaining long-term positivity doesn't happen by accident—it requires a thoughtful, structured approach. A personal action plan helps you stay on track, even when life gets tough. Let's explore how to build a concrete strategy for maintaining positivity in your day-to-day life.

1. Set Clear Intentions for Positivity

Before you can achieve any goal, you need to define what success looks like. What does a positive life mean to you? How will you know when you're consistently living in a positive mindset?

- **Be specific**: Your intention might be to experience more joy, practice more gratitude, or reduce the amount of negative self-talk. Make it tangible, such as "I will write down three things I'm grateful for every day" or "I will respond with calmness when faced with challenges."
- **Review and revise**: Your intentions may evolve over time as you grow. Revisit them regularly to ensure they still align

with your goals and adjust them as needed.

2. Develop Positive Daily Routines

Your daily habits are the building blocks of a positive mindset. Implementing routines that reinforce positivity helps create a strong foundation.

- **Morning routines for positivity**: How you start your day often dictates how the rest of the day will go. Start with practices like meditation, gratitude journaling, or reading something inspiring. Set a positive tone before diving into work or life's demands.
- **Evening reflection**: End each day with reflection. Consider what went well, what challenges you faced, and how you handled them. This practice reinforces self-awareness and helps you see your growth over time.

3. Create a Support System for Accountability

It's easier to stay positive when you have a support network that encourages and uplifts you.

- **Identify positive influences**: Surround yourself with people who inspire and motivate you. Share your goals with friends, family, or mentors who will help hold you accountable for maintaining a positive mindset.
- **Join communities with similar goals**: Look for groups—whether online or in person—where positivity and self-improvement are core values. This could include a mastermind group, a positivity-focused online forum, or a meditation circle.

4. Track Your Progress and Adjust When Necessary

A personal action plan should be dynamic and flexible, allowing you to make adjustments as you grow.

- **Keep a positivity journal**: Write down your thoughts, experiences, and any shifts in mindset. Documenting your journey helps you see patterns and celebrate small wins.
- **Be adaptable**: If something in your plan isn't working, don't hesitate to change it. Positivity isn't about rigidity but about staying true to your goals in a way that serves your growth.

The Role of Continuous Self-Improvement and Reflection

Self-improvement and reflection are essential components of

Shifting Mindsets

sustaining a long-term positive mindset. Growth fuels positivity, and self-awareness helps you stay aligned with your goals.

1. Commit to Lifelong Learning

One of the most powerful ways to maintain positivity is through continuous growth. Whether you're improving your emotional intelligence, learning a new skill, or expanding your knowledge, learning keeps your mind active and open.

- **Expand your emotional intelligence**: Understanding your emotions and those of others leads to better relationships and a more grounded mindset. Take time to study emotional intelligence and apply it in your personal and professional life.
- **Embrace new experiences**: Stepping out of your comfort zone fosters resilience and growth. Take on challenges that excite you or push you to grow, whether that's learning a new language, taking up a hobby, or pursuing a passion project.

2. Reflect Regularly on Your Progress

Reflection is a powerful tool for self-awareness and growth. It helps you stay connected to your goals and gives your insight into areas for improvement.

- **Practice regular self-reflection**: Set aside time each week or month to reflect on your mindset and actions. Ask yourself questions like: What went well? What challenges did I face? How can I improve moving forward?
- **Celebrate progress, no matter how small**: Recognize that even small steps forward are wins. Celebrating your progress fosters motivation and helps you maintain a positive outlook.

3. Adapt a Growth Mindset

A growth mindset is the belief that you can improve and develop through effort, learning, and perseverance. This mindset is essential for sustaining positivity because it allows you to see challenges as opportunities for growth rather than obstacles.

- **Reframe challenges as learning experiences**: Instead of seeing mistakes as failures, view them as opportunities to learn and grow. This mindset keeps you focused on progress rather than setbacks.
- **Set goals that push you**: Stretch yourself with goals that challenge you to grow. Whether they're related to career,

Shifting Mindsets

personal development, or relationships, choose goals that require effort and dedication.

Staying Motivated and Consistent in the Journey toward Positivity

Positivity is a lifelong journey, not a destination. It's essential to stay motivated and consistent, even when the path feels difficult. Here's how to maintain your drive toward a positive mindset.

1. Find Your "Why"

Understanding your deeper motivation for positivity is crucial for staying the course. Why do you want to live a more positive life? Is it to improve your relationships, reduce stress, or enhance your overall well-being?

- **Identify your core motivation**: When you understand your deeper reasons for seeking positivity, it becomes easier to stay focused on that goal. For example, if you want more fulfilling relationships, remind yourself how positivity enhances connection.
- **Use your "why" as fuel**: Whenever you face challenges or setbacks, revisit your "why." This serves as a reminder of the long-term benefits of maintaining a positive mindset.

2. Break down Big Goals into Small, Achievable Steps

Sometimes, the journey to long-term positivity can feel overwhelming, especially if you're just starting out.

Breaking your goals down into smaller steps makes them more manageable and keeps you motivated.

- **Set small, incremental goals**: Instead of aiming to "be positive all the time," break it down into achievable goals. For example, "I will practice gratitude every morning" or "I will replace one negative thought with a positive one each day."
- **Celebrate milestones**: As you achieve each small step, take time to acknowledge your progress. This reinforces positive behaviour and helps you stay motivated for the long haul.

3. Stay Accountable with Regular Check-Ins

Having accountability helps ensure you stay consistent. Whether it's through a friend, coach, or personal system, check-ins keep you aligned with your goals.

- **Schedule regular check-ins**: Every week or month, set aside time to

4. Incorporate Positivity into Your Environment

Your physical surroundings can significantly impact your mindset. Creating an environment that fosters positivity helps make it a natural part of your lifestyle.

- **Declutter your space**: A clean, organized space can promote clarity and reduce stress. Take time to de-clutter your home and workspace. Surround yourself with items that inspire and uplift you—photos of loved ones, motivational quotes, or artwork that resonates with you.
- **Use uplifting colours and scents**: Colours and scents can influence mood. Consider painting your walls in calming colours or incorporating bright, cheerful hues. Essential oils, fresh flowers, or scented candles can create an inviting atmosphere that enhances positivity.

5. Practice Kindness and Compassion

Positivity often extends beyond the self; it can be cultivated through acts of kindness and compassion toward others. When you contribute positively to others' lives, it enhances your sense of fulfilment and happiness.

- **Engage in random acts of kindness**: Simple gestures—like holding the door for someone, paying a compliment, or helping a neighbour—can create a ripple effect of positivity. These acts reinforce your positive mindset and inspire others to do the same.
- **Volunteer in your community**: Giving your time and energy to help others can bring immense joy and satisfaction. Find a cause you're passionate about and volunteer regularly. This not only helps those in need but also enhances your sense of purpose and belonging.

Creating a Personal Action Plan for Maintaining a Positive Mindset (Continued)

1. Leverage Technology for Positivity

In today's digital world, technology can be a powerful ally in maintaining positivity.

- **Use apps for mindfulness and positivity**: Numerous apps can assist in your journey—meditation apps like Headspace or Calm, gratitude journals like Five Minute Journal, or motivational quote apps that inspire daily. Incorporate these into your routine for added support.

Shifting Mindsets

- **Follow positive content online**: Curate your social media feeds to include uplifting, inspirational content. Follow accounts that promote positivity, personal growth, and encouragement. Be mindful of how social media affects your mood and adjust your exposure accordingly.

2. Maintain a Positive Network

Your social circle is a crucial component of your action plan for positivity. Relationships can either uplift or drain you, so being intentional about your connections is vital.

- **Conduct a relationship inventory**: Reflect on your relationships and how they impact your well-being. Are there individuals who consistently bring you down? Consider limiting your time with them while seeking out more uplifting connections.
- **Engage in supportive activities**: Plan regular get-togethers with friends who share your positivity goals. Whether it's a book club focused on personal development or a walking group, engaging in positive activities reinforces your commitment to a positive mindset.

3. Practice Self-Compassion

As you embark on your journey of self-improvement, it's essential to approach yourself with kindness and understanding.

- **Acknowledge imperfections**: Everyone has flaws and makes mistakes; it's part of being human. Embrace your imperfections as opportunities for growth rather than sources of shame.
- **Engage in positive self-talk**: Shift your inner dialogue to one of encouragement and support. Replace self-critical thoughts with affirmations that acknowledge your efforts and potential.

4. Seek Feedback for Growth

Constructive feedback is a valuable tool for self-improvement.

- **Be open to receiving feedback**: Whether from friends, colleagues, or mentors, welcome feedback as a way to learn and grow. Create a culture of open communication in your relationships where sharing constructive feedback is encouraged.
- **Implement feedback for improvement**: After receiving feedback, take time to reflect on it. Identify specific steps you can take to implement suggestions and demonstrate

your commitment to growth.

Staying Motivated and Consistent in the Journey toward Positivity (Continued)

1. Embrace a Flexible Mindset

Life is full of changes and uncertainties; a flexible mindset helps you adapt without losing your positivity.

- **Be open to change**: Understand that change can be a catalyst for growth. Embrace new experiences, even if they take you out of your comfort zone. The ability to adapt can enhance your resilience and keep your positivity intact.
- **View challenges as opportunities**: Instead of fearing challenges, see them as chances to learn. Cultivating a mindset that frames difficulties as opportunities can maintain your positivity even in adversity.

2. Create a "Positivity Playlist"

Music can profoundly affect mood. Curating a playlist filled with songs that inspire and uplift you can serve as a quick source of positivity.

- **Choose empowering songs**: Select tracks that resonate with you, promoting feelings of joy, hope, and motivation. Listening to this playlist during challenging moments can shift your mindset and provide a quick emotional boost.
- **Explore different genres**: Don't limit yourself to one genre. Explore various styles, from upbeat pop to calming classical, to find what uplifts you most effectively.

3. Utilize Visualization Techniques

Visualization is a powerful technique used by many successful individuals to maintain a positive mindset and achieve their goals.

- **Create a vision board**: Gather images, quotes, and symbols that represent your goals and the positive life you aspire to live. Display your vision board in a prominent place where you can see it daily, serving as a constant reminder of your journey.
- **Practice guided imagery**: Set aside time to close your eyes and visualize yourself achieving your goals. Picture the emotions and sensations associated with your success. This practice reinforces your commitment to positivity and keeps your goals front and centre.

4. Engage in Physical Activity

Physical health is intricately linked to mental well-being. Regular exercise releases endorphins, which naturally boost mood and promote positivity.

- **Find an enjoyable activity**: Whether it's dancing, hiking, yoga, or swimming, choose activities that you enjoy. When you find joy in movement, you're more likely to incorporate it into your routine.
- **Incorporate movement into your daily life**: Even small changes, like taking the stairs instead of the elevator or going for a walk during breaks, can enhance your overall positivity and mental clarity.

Sustaining long-term positivity is a multi-layered process that involves intentional actions, self-awareness, and community support. By understanding that positivity is a lifestyle choice, creating an actionable plan, embracing continuous self-improvement, and staying motivated, you can cultivate a lasting positive mindset. Remember that the journey toward positivity is ongoing and unique to you. Embrace it with an open heart and a willingness to grow, and you will find not only a happier life but also the ability to inspire others on their paths to positivity.

CHAPTER 10. LIVING A PURPOSE-DRIVEN LIFE

Living a purpose-driven life is about aligning your actions, mindset, and values with a deeper sense of meaning that guides you daily. This chapter explores how a positive mindset enhances your ability to discover and live in alignment with your purpose. By weaving positivity into every aspect of life, you create a fulfilling, balanced existence where success and happiness go hand-in-hand. Let's dive into how you can make this shift toward a purpose-driven, positive life.

Aligning Your Mindset with Your Life's Purpose and Values

At the heart of living a purpose-driven life is a profound alignment between what you believe, what you value, and how you act. It's about walking the path that resonates most deeply with who you are, not just following societal expectations or external pressures. A purpose-driven life is one where each decision, whether small or large, is informed by your values and the broader mission you believe in. Here's how to align your mindset with your life's purpose:

1. Reflect Deeply on Your Core Values Your values are the guiding principles that shape how you live your life. When your mindset and actions are in sync with these core values, you'll experience more internal harmony. To start:

- **Identify Your Core Beliefs**: Take time to reflect on what matters most to you. Ask yourself, "What do I believe in? What principles would I defend, no matter what?" These values might include honesty, growth, creativity, or kindness.
- **Evaluate Your Current Mindset**: Once you identify your core beliefs, evaluate whether your current mindset supports these values. For example, if one of your values is compassion, is your daily inner dialogue kind and compassionate toward yourself and others? Realigning your thoughts to support your values is crucial for authentic living.

2. Set Clear, Purpose-Driven Goals Living purposefully means your actions have direction. It's important to set goals that not only

reflect what you want to achieve but also align with the bigger picture of your life. To ensure alignment:
- **Ask Purposeful Questions**: When setting goals, ask yourself questions like, "Does this goal reflect who I am? Will achieving this help me serve a greater purpose?" This level of introspection ensures that your ambitions are rooted in what truly matters to you.
- **Reframe Obstacles as Learning Opportunities**: When aligned with your purpose, setbacks no longer feel like dead ends. Instead, they become valuable learning experiences. Every challenge can be reframed to help you grow closer to your purpose. This shift in perspective is the bedrock of a purpose-driven mindset.

3. Regularly Reassess Your Alignment Living a purpose-driven life isn't a static experience—it requires regular reassessment. As you grow and evolve, your understanding of your purpose may deepen, and your values might shift. To stay aligned:
- **Practice Reflection and Journaling**: Incorporate reflection into your routine. Journaling is an excellent way to check in with yourself, assess whether your current actions align with your purpose, and recalibrate where necessary.
- **Embrace Change as Part of the Journey**: Recognize that living a purpose-driven life is a dynamic process. As you discover new facets of your identity and purpose, be open to shifting your goals and mindset to stay true to the evolving you.

How a Positive Mindset Can Help You Discover and Pursue Your Passion

A positive mindset is a powerful tool for discovering your passions and living in alignment with them. Positivity not only fuels your desire to explore new opportunities but also gives you the resilience to navigate the inevitable challenges that come with pursuing your passion.

1. Cultivate Curiosity and Open-Mindedness Discovering your passion begins with curiosity. A positive mindset encourages you to approach life with a sense of wonder and openness. When you're positive:
- **You Explore without Fear of Failure**: A positive mindset

allows you to try new things without the paralyzing fear of failure. You begin to see failure as a stepping stone to success rather than something to avoid.
- **You See Opportunities Everywhere**: Positivity opens your mind to see potential in places you might have overlooked. Instead of focusing on limitations, you focus on possibilities, creating a fertile environment for your passions to flourish.

2. Overcome Limiting Beliefs

Many people struggle to pursue their passions because of limiting beliefs—those deeply ingrained thoughts that tell you "I can't" or "I'm not enough." A positive mindset challenges and dismantles these limiting beliefs by helping you focus on your strengths and potential.

- **Affirm Your Capabilities**: Positive affirmations can rewire your thinking, allowing you to believe in your ability to pursue your passion. Statements like "I am capable of achieving my dreams" or "I have the skills to find my purpose" help reframe your thinking.
- **Focus on Growth over Perfection**: A positive mindset shifts your focus from needing to be perfect to embracing growth. When you approach your passion with a growth mindset, you allow yourself room to make mistakes and learn from them, fuelling continuous improvement.

3. Stay Resilient Through Challenges

Pursuing your passion is not always easy. There will be challenges along the way that test your resolve. A positive mindset provides the resilience needed to keep going when the road gets tough.

- **Harness the Power of Optimism**: Optimism, a key component of positivity, enables you to believe in a better future even when the present is difficult. By focusing on what can go right rather than what can go wrong, you maintain momentum and enthusiasm for your passion.
- **Practice Patience and Persistence**: Passion-driven work takes time. A positive mindset helps you stay patient and persistent, understanding that success doesn't happen overnight, but with consistent effort and belief in yourself.

Shifting Mindsets

Strategies for Integrating Positivity into All Aspects of Your Life

To live a truly positive, purpose-driven life, positivity must permeate every aspect of your existence—work, relationships, personal growth, and even how you interact with the world around you. Here's how to integrate positivity holistically:

1. Cultivate Positivity at Work

Whether you're working in your dream job or something that simply pays the bills, cultivating positivity in the workplace is key to overall happiness.

- **Create a Positive Work Environment**: Start by fostering a positive attitude in your own workspace. Surround yourself with things that motivate you—whether it's personal mementos, inspiring quotes, or creating a clutter-free, organized desk. Positivity in your physical space translates into a more positive mindset.
- **Adopt a Solutions-Oriented Mindset**: In challenging work situations, positivity helps you focus on solutions instead of problems. When confronted with obstacles, ask yourself, "What can I do to make this better?" instead of fixating on what's wrong.

2. Build Positive, Fulfilling Relationships

Relationships, both personal and professional, play a significant role in your happiness. Integrating positivity into your interactions with others helps foster stronger, more meaningful connections.

- **Communicate with Empathy and Encouragement**: In your relationships, practice listening with empathy and offering words of encouragement. Positivity isn't about ignoring problems, but addressing them constructively with kindness.
- **Set Boundaries to Protect Your Positivity**: While it's important to maintain positive relationships, it's equally essential to set boundaries with those who drain your energy. Limit your exposure to negativity and protect your emotional well-being.

3. Practice Self-Positivity in Personal Growth

Your relationship with yourself is foundational to how you live your life. Practicing self-positivity is about cultivating a mindset that nurtures your growth and well-being.

- **Celebrate Small Wins**: Incorporate positivity into your

self-growth journey by celebrating even the smallest achievements. Recognizing progress boosts your confidence and keeps you motivated to continue evolving.
- **Practice Self-Love and Forgiveness**: Be kind to yourself during difficult times. A positive mindset helps you forgive yourself for mistakes and move forward with a renewed sense of purpose.

Final Thoughts: Positivity as an Ongoing Journey

Positivity isn't a one-time achievement; it's a continuous, evolving journey. Living a purpose-driven life means staying committed to nurturing positivity in all areas—work, relationships, personal development, and beyond. Here's how to make positivity an ongoing part of your life:

1. Embrace Lifelong Learning and Growth

Staying positive and purpose-driven requires an ongoing commitment to learning and growth. View every experience, good or bad, as an opportunity for personal development. With each step forward, you gain deeper insights into yourself and your purpose.

2. Surround Yourself with Positive Influences

To sustain positivity, it's essential to curate an environment—physical, emotional, and social—that reinforces your positive mindset. Surround yourself with people, ideas, and experiences that uplift and inspire you.

3. Stay Mindful of Your Energy

Positivity requires energy, both mental and physical. Regularly check in with yourself to ensure you're investing your energy in things that align with your values and bring you joy. Prioritize self-care and rest to keep your positive mindset thriving.

Living a purpose-driven life, fuelled by positivity, is a transformative experience. It allows you to navigate challenges with grace, pursue your passions fearlessly, and build a life that's not only successful but also deeply meaningful. As you continue this journey, remember that positivity is not a destination but a way of living—one that evolves and grows with you, shaping a life of fulfilment, joy, and purpose

Transitioning from stable employment to venturing out on your own—whether it's changing jobs or starting your own business—is one of the most significant decisions anyone can make. It's a shift that brings both challenges and opportunities. This decision comes with the potential for great rewards, including personal growth, financial independence, and the freedom to shape your life according to your values. However, it also carries risks, as leaving a stable job often means stepping into the unknown, embracing uncertainty, and learning how to trust in your abilities more than ever before.

I've worked with numerous individuals who've made this transition, and I've seen how it can profoundly impact all aspects of life—from career satisfaction to family dynamics and personal fulfilment. In this piece, I'll explore the challenges of leaving stable employment, the mindset shifts required for success, and the powerful, positive effects that being your own boss can have on your life, your family, and your overall sense of well-being.

The Difficulty of Transitioning from Stable Employment
Comfort vs. Growth

Stable employment offers security, a regular pay check, predictable hours, and a certain level of comfort. For many, this stability creates a sense of certainty, which can be comforting, especially if you have a family depending on you. However, this comfort can also act as a trap, preventing you from realizing your full potential. Psychologically, humans are wired to seek security, but true growth comes from stepping outside of your comfort zone. The fear of losing stability can be one of the biggest barriers to leaving a job, even when you know deep down that you're capable of more.

Mindset Shift: To make this transition successfully, you need to reframe your thinking. Instead of viewing stability as the ultimate goal, recognize that uncertainty can bring opportunities for personal and professional growth. Growth requires discomfort, and by stepping into the unknown, you allow yourself the chance to expand your skills, challenge your limits, and find new paths to success.

Fear of Failure

Another significant obstacle is the fear of failure. In stable employment, even if the work is uninspiring or not aligned with your passion, the structure is familiar. Venturing out to change jobs or start your own business requires taking on new responsibilities, learning new skills, and sometimes failing along the way. The fear of not succeeding in your new venture can be paralyzing and often keeps people anchored in roles they've outgrown.

Mindset Shift: Rather than seeing failure as something to avoid, embrace it as a natural part of the journey toward success. Every successful entrepreneur and career changer has experienced setbacks. What sets them apart is their ability to learn from these experiences, adapt, and keep moving forward. Failure is simply feedback, a stepping stone that brings you closer to your goal.

Financial Uncertainty

Financial insecurity is another common concern when considering leaving a stable job. The prospect of inconsistent income, especially if you're starting a new business, can be daunting. Many people have mortgages, car payments, and family expenses to consider, which makes financial risk feel even greater. However, the fear of financial instability can be addressed with careful planning and preparation.

Mindset Shift: Approach financial uncertainty with a strategic mindset. Before making the leap, save an emergency fund that can cover several months of expenses. Additionally, explore side hustles or freelance work to create supplementary income streams while you build your new venture. Seeing financial uncertainty as a manageable challenge rather than an insurmountable barrier can help ease the transition.

The Positive Impact of Being Your Own Boss

While the transition may come with challenges, the rewards of being your own boss are life-changing. Whether you're starting your own business or simply seeking more autonomy in your career, the freedom, fulfilment, and control you gain over your life can bring transformative benefits.

Personal Freedom and Flexibility

One of the most obvious benefits of being your own boss is the freedom to set your own schedule. No more being confined by the rigid 9-to-5 routine or being told when you can take a vacation. Instead, you have the power to design a work-life balance that fits your needs and priorities. Want to spend more time with your children, pursue a hobby, or travel while working? When you run your own business or manage your career independently, you can structure your life around these desires.

For many, the flexibility to attend a child's school event, take time for self-care, or simply enjoy more leisure time without needing approval from a boss is invaluable. This sense of control over your time leads to greater life satisfaction and a deeper sense of fulfilment.

Increased Financial Potential

Although the transition to self-employment or entrepreneurship can

Shifting Mindsets

bring short-term financial uncertainty, it also opens up the potential for significant financial growth in the long term. When you're working for yourself, there are no salary caps or limits to what you can earn. Your income is directly tied to your efforts, skills, and the value you bring to the marketplace.

Many entrepreneurs find that after an initial adjustment period, they're able to far surpass the income they made in traditional employment. This is particularly true for individuals who build scalable businesses that allow them to increase their revenue without directly trading their time for money.

Mindset Shift: Instead of seeing the financial risk, focus on the potential financial freedom that comes with being your own boss. It may take time to reach your income goals, but with persistence, smart planning, and a focus on growth, the potential is limitless.

Greater Control over Your Career

When you work for someone else, your career path is often dictated by external factors—your employer's goals, organizational changes, or the availability of promotions. By venturing out on your own, you take full control of your career. You get to decide which projects to pursue, which clients to work with, and what direction your business will take.

This level of autonomy can lead to a deeper sense of professional fulfilment because you're building something that's entirely your own. You can align your work with your passions, values, and long-term goals. Instead of feeling stuck in a job that doesn't excite you, you have the opportunity to create a career that brings you joy and purpose.

Positive Impact on Your Family

Being your own boss doesn't just benefit you—it can also have a profound positive impact on your family. When you have more control over your time and finances, you can be more present with your loved ones. Whether it's attending important family events, being there for your children's milestones, or simply having more quality time together, the flexibility of self-employment allows you to prioritize your family in ways that traditional employment may not.

Additionally, as your business grows, it can become a family asset. Many entrepreneurs involve their spouses or children in their business, turning it into a shared venture that brings the family closer together and creates a legacy for future generations.

Shifting Mindsets

Building Confidence and Resilience

Stepping into the world of self-employment or entrepreneurship requires resilience, determination, and self-belief. Overcoming the challenges of building a business or forging a new career path builds character and strengthens your sense of self-worth. The personal growth you experience as you navigate obstacles and solve problems will make you more confident in every area of your life.

Mindset Shift: Instead of waiting for permission from others to pursue your dreams, recognize that you have the power to create the life you want. Trusting in your abilities and taking ownership of your success leads to an unshakable confidence that impacts not just your professional life but your personal relationships, health, and overall happiness.

A Sense of Purpose

One of the greatest rewards of working for yourself is the ability to align your work with your passions and values. Whether you're starting a business that solves a problem you're passionate about or transitioning into a career that aligns with your personal values, the sense of purpose that comes from doing meaningful work is unmatched.

When you feel that your work is making a positive impact—whether on your clients, community, or industry—you'll experience a sense of fulfilment that goes far beyond financial success. This sense of purpose can become a driving force that keeps you motivated, even during tough times.

The transition from stable employment to working for yourself is not without its challenges, but the rewards far outweigh the risks. The opportunity to create a life filled with freedom, purpose, and financial independence is within reach for those who are willing to take the leap. By embracing a growth mindset, facing fears head-on, and committing to personal and professional growth, you can successfully navigate this transition and enjoy the countless benefits of being your own boss.

Whether you're seeking more flexibility, financial freedom, or the chance to pursue your passions, the decision to leave stable employment and venture out on your own can be one of the most empowering choices you'll ever make—one that has the potential to positively transform not just your career, but your entire life.

Shifting Mindsets

Bonus Section: Workbook and Exercises

This section is designed to be your personal guide for turning the lessons of this book into real-life action. As a professional life coach, I believe that transformation happens through consistent, small steps. These exercises will help you solidify the changes you're making and keep you on track toward your goal of cultivating a positive mindset. Take your time with each exercise, and revisit them often as you grow and evolve on your journey!

Guided Journaling Prompts

Journaling is one of the most powerful tools for self-reflection and growth. Use these prompts to gain clarity, explore your emotions, and deepen your understanding of your current mindset.

1. **What negative thoughts or beliefs hold me back the most?**
   - Identify recurring thoughts that keep you stuck. Reflect on their origins and the role they play in your life.
2. **When do I feel the most positive and empowered?**
   - Think about situations, people, or activities that boost your mood and energy. How can you invite more of these into your life?
3. **What's one thing I can do today to shift my perspective toward positivity?**
   - Small actions lead to big changes. Write down a simple action step you can take today to focus on the positive.
4. **What challenges have I overcome in the past, and what strengths did I use?**
   - Reflect on past successes and the inner strengths that helped you through tough times. Acknowledge your resilience.
5. **How do I want to feel daily, and what can I do to support that feeling?**
   - Define the emotions you want to experience daily and identify the habits or routines that can help you feel that way.

Daily Affirmations

Affirmations are positive statements that challenge negative thoughts and reinforce new beliefs. Repeat these daily or create your own to align with your personal goals.

Shifting Mindsets

- "I am capable of handling anything that comes my way."
- "I choose to focus on what I can control and let go of what I cannot."
- "Every day, I am becoming the person I want to be."
- "I embrace challenges as opportunities to learn and grow."
- "Positivity flows through me, and I attract good energy into my life."

Pro Tip: Place these affirmations where you'll see them often—on your bathroom mirror, desk, or phone background. Consistency is key!

Gratitude Log Template

Gratitude is one of the simplest and most effective ways to shift your mindset. Use this template to create a daily habit of appreciating the good in your life.

Date	Three Things I Am Grateful For	Why They Matter To Me
Example: Oct 22	1. My supportive family	They help me through tough times.
	2. The sunshine today	It boosts my mood and energy.
	3. Learning something new	It keeps me growing and inspired.

Pro Tip: Spend just 5 minutes each morning or night reflecting on what you're grateful for. It will help you start or end your day with a positive mindset.

Mindset Tracking Sheet

Tracking your progress is essential to creating lasting change. Use this sheet to monitor your mindset shifts and see the positive patterns develop over time.

Week	Positive Actions	How I Felt	How I Felt	What I Learned

Shifting Mindsets

	Taken	Before	After	
Week 1 (Oct 22)	Practiced affirmations	Anxious	Calmer, more focused	I can control my mindset.

Pro Tip: Review your tracking sheet every week. Celebrate your wins, no matter how small. Acknowledging progress builds momentum!

Suggested Reading and Resources for Continued Growth

Here are some highly recommended books, podcasts, and online resources to continue expanding your mindset toward positivity and personal development:

Books:
1. **"The Power of Now" by Eckhart Tolle** – A deep dive into living in the present moment and letting go of negative thought patterns.
2. **"Atomic Habits" by James Clear** – Practical strategies for building positive habits and breaking negative ones.
3. **"The Four Agreements" by Don Miguel Ruiz** – A simple but profound guide to living with more freedom, happiness, and positivity.

Podcasts:
1. **The Mindvalley Podcast** – Features interviews with top personal growth experts on topics ranging from mindset to self-improvement.
2. **The Tim Ferriss Show** – Interviews with high achievers on their habits, routines, and life philosophies.
3. **Oprah's SuperSoul Conversations** – Conversations with thought leaders on spirituality, self-reflection, and inner peace.

Online Resources:
1. **Headspace** (App) – A meditation and mindfulness app to help you manage stress and cultivate a positive mindset.
2. **TED Talks** – Inspirational and educational talks on mindset, personal growth, and success.

3. **Mindvalley Academy** – An online personal growth platform offering courses on mindset, health, and well-being.

Final Words of Encouragement
Remember, changing your mindset is a journey, not a destination. It's about making small, consistent choices each day that lead to a more positive, fulfilled life. Be patient with yourself, celebrate your progress, and embrace the growth you're experiencing. You've got this! Keep going, and never forget how powerful your mindset can be in shaping your reality.

Good Luck, you've got this.

Craig Howarth

www.ingramcontent.com/pod-product-compliance
Lightning Source LLC
Chambersburg PA
CBHW070236220526
45465CB00004B/1441